Production Grids in Asia

T0180928

Simon C. Lin • Eric Yen
Editors

Production Grids in Asia

Applications, Developments and Global Ties

 Springer

Editors
Simon C. Lin
Academia Sinica
Grid Computing Center
128 Sec. Academia Road
Taipei 115
Nankang
Taiwan R.O.C.
Simon.Lin@twgrid.org

Eric Yen
Academia Sinica
Grid Computing Center
128 Sec. Academia Road
Taipei 115
Nankang
Taiwan R.O.C.
Eric.Yen@twgrid.org

ISBN 978-1-4899-8439-5   ISBN 978-1-4419-0046-3 (eBook)
DOI 10.1007/978-1-4419-0046-3
Springer New York Dordrecht Heidelberg London

Printed on acid-free paper

Springer is part of Springer Science+Business Media (www.springer.com)

Contents

Part I Grid Activities in Asia Pacific

Chapter 1
Asia Federation Report International Symposium on Grid Computing 2008
Simon C. Lin, Min Tsai & Eric Yen (ASGC, Taiwan)   3

Chapter 2
Grid Operation at Tokyo Tier-2 Centre for Atlas
Hiroyuki Matsunaga (KEK, Japan)   29

Chapter 3
The EUAsiaGrid Project
Marco Paganoni (University of Milano-Bicocca and INFN, Italy)   41

Part II Applications – High Energy Physics, Biomedicine & Life Sciences, Humanities & Social Sciences, Digital Library & Content Management and Earth Science

Chapter 4
The e-Science for High Energy Physics in Korea
Kihyeon Cho (KISTI, Korea)   49

Chapter5
CMS Data Transfer Tests in Preparation to LHC Data-Taking
Daniele Bonacorsi (INFN-CNAF, Italy)   59

Chapter 6
CMS Computing Operations at INFN-CNAF with Castor MSS
Daniele Bonacorsi, Andrea Sartirana, Luca Dell'Agnello, Pier Paolo Ricci &
Dejan Vitlacil (INFN-CNAF, Bologna, Italy)   71

Chapter 7
Distributed Computing and Data Analysis for CMS in View of the LHC Startup
Peter Kreuzer (RWTH-Aachen IIIa, Switzerland)   79

Chapter 8

Grid Technologies for Cancer Research in the ACGT Project

Juliusz Pukacki (Poznan Supercomputing and Networking Centre, Poland)

93

Chapter 9

Secure Grid Services for Cooperative Work in Medicine and Life Science

Anette Weisbecker (Fraunhofer IAO, Germany)

107

Chapter 10

From tools and services to e-Infrastructure for the arts and humanities

Tobias Blanke (King's College London, United Kingdom)

117

Chapter 11

Digital library storage in an iRODS data grid

Mark Hedges (King's College London, UK)   129

Chapter 12

Architectural Design for GRID Clearinghouse Service

Johannes K. Chiang & Kiekang Chao

(Dept. of MIS, National Cheng-Chi University, Taiwan)   141

Part III   Grid Middleware & Interoperability

Chapter 13

Interoperability between gLite and GOS

Yaodong Cheng (Chinese Academy of Sciences, China)   155

Chapter 14

Realizing Inter-operability among Grids: A Case Study with GARUDA Grid and the EGEE Grid

Shamjith K. V. (Centre for Development of Advanced Computing/C-DAC, India)   175

Chapter 15

Uniform Access to Heterogeneous Grid Infrastructures with JSAGA

Sylvain Reynaud (IN2P3/CNRS, France)   185

Part IV   *Operation & Management*

Chapter 16

Development and Operation of the D-Grid Infrastructure
Thomas Fieseler (Jülich Supercomputing Centre, Germany)   199

Program Committee

(In Last Name Alphabetic Order)

Eileen Berman
Fermi National Accelerator
Laboratory
USA

Ian Bird
CERN
CH

Kors Bos
NIKHEF
NL

Fabrizio Gagliardi
Microsoft
USA

Robert Jones (Chair)
EGEE
CH

Setsuya Kawabata
KEK
JP

Yannick Legre
Healthgrid
FR

Simon C. Lin
Academia Sinica
TW

Ludek Matyska
CESNET
CZ

Klaus-Peter Mickel
FZK
DE

Glenn R. Moloney
University of Melbourne
AU

Reagan Moore
SDSC
USA

Marco Paganoni
INFN
IT

Ruth Pordes
Fermi National Accelerator
Laboratory
USA

Peter Rice
European Bioinformatics Institute
UK

Leslie Robertson
CERN
CH

Hiroshi Sakamoto
University of Tokyo
JP

Takashi Sasaki
KEK
JP

Pansak Siriruchatapong
NECTEC
TH

Dane Skow
Argonne National Laboratory
and University of Chicago
USA

Alexander Voss
NCeSS, University of Man-
chester
UK

Vicky White
Fermi National Accelerator
Laboratory
USA

Lawrence Wong
National University of Singa-
pore
SG

Bao-ping Yan
Chinese Academy of Science
CN

Contributors

- **Asvija B**
  Centre for Development of Advanced Computing (C-DAC), India
- **Prahlada Rao B**
  Centre for Development of Advanced Computing (C-DAC), India
- **Tobias Blanke**
  Centre for e-Research/ Arts and Humanities Data Service,
  King's College London, United Kingdom
- **Daniele Bonacorsi**
  University of Bologna (on behalf of the CMS Collaboration), Italy
- **Kiekang Chao**
  Dept. of MIS, National Cheng-Chi University, Taiwan
- **Gang Chen**
  Institute of High Energy Physics, Chinese Academy of Sciences, China
- **Yaodong Cheng**
  Institute of High Energy Physics, Chinese Academy of Sciences, China
- **Johannes K. Chiang**
  Dept. of MIS, National Cheng-Chi University, Taiwan
- **Kihyeon Cho**
  Korea Institute of Science and Technology Information (KISTI), Korea
- **Jürgen Falkner**
  Fraunhofer IAO, Germany
- **Thomas Fieseler**
  Jülich Supercomputing Centre, Germany
- **Wolfgang Gürich**
  Jülich Supercomputing Centre, Germany
- **Adil Hasan**
  Department of English, Liverpool University, United Kingdom
- **Fraunhofer Iais**
  Poznan Supercomputing and Networking Centre, Germany
- **Tadaaki Isobe**
  International Centre for Elementary Particle Physics,
  the University of Tokyo, Japan
- **Hyunwoo Kim**
  Korea Institute of Science and Technology Information (KISTI), Korea
- **Shamjith KV**
  Centre for Development of Advanced Computing (C-DAC), India
- **Simon C. Lin**
  Academia Sinica, Taiwan

- **Tetsuro Mashimo**
  International Centre for Elementary Particle Physics,
  the University of Tokyo,   Japan
- **Hiroyuki Matsunaga**
  International Centre for Elementary Particle Physics,
  the University of Tokyo,   Japan
- **Mohanram N**
  Centre for Development of Advanced Computing (C-DAC),   India
- **Juliusz Pukacki1**
  Poznan Supercomputing and Networking Centre,   Poland
- **Sridharan R**
  Centre for Development of Advanced Computing (C-DAC),   India
- **Sylvain Reynaud**
  CNRS/IN2P3 Computing Centre,   France
- **Hiroshi Sakamoto**
  International Centre for Elementary Particle Physics,
  the University of Tokyo,   Japan
- **Min Tsai**
  Academia Sinica Grid Computing Centre   Taiwan
- **Ikuo Ueda**
  International Centre for Elementary Particle Physics,
  the University of Tokyo,   Japan
- **Yongjian Wang**
  Institute of High Energy Physics, Chinese Academy of Sciences,   China
- **Anette Weisbecker**
  Fraunhofer IAO,   Germany
- **Eric Yen**
  Academia Sinica,   Taiwan

Part I   Grid Activities in Asia Pacific

Asia Federation Report International Symposium on Grid Computing 2008

Simon C. Lin, Min Tsai & Eric Yen

Academia Sinica Grid Computing Centre, Taiwan

1. Introduction

The focus of this report is to capture to provide a summary of developments in Asia-Pacific region from the International Symposium on Grid Computing 2008. This document contains three sections. The first section provides a status update of EGEE activities in the region. This is followed by ideas for further extending EGEE III into Asia-Pacific. The third section contains a short description of networking, Grid and EGEE involvement for each country.

2. EGEE Status in Asia

Applications

Asia-Pacific resource centers used 624 KSI2K years of computing resource compared to 200 KSI2K years in the previous year. LHC experiments and Biomed are still the major applications in Asia pacific (80.13%), but usage by Belle (9.81%) and CDF(9.99%) continue to increase.

S.C. Lin and E. Yen (eds.), *Production Grids in Asia: Applications, Developments and Global Ties*, DOI 10.1007/978-1-4419-0046-3_1,
© Springer Science + Business Media, LLC 2010

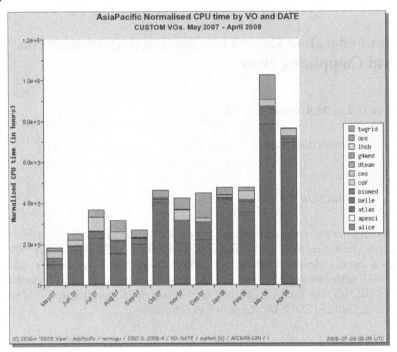

Based on the solid foundation established by drug discovery achievements from 2006, the Avian Flu project was not only lead to insightful scientific results, but also initiated vigorous efforts to generalize the virtual screening e-Science services. A generalized virtual screening service would facilitate the widespread deployment of grid application and ease-of-use. Development in this area will be integrated with NA4 in EGEE III in collaboration with other partners.

Operations

EGEE and ASGC have established the Asia-Pacific Regional Operations Center (APROC) since April of 2005. The mission of APROC is to provide operations support in the regional to facilitate the expansion of the Grid and maximize the availability of Grid services that are available. APROC provides deployment, operation, regional CA and contributes to global operations support for EGEE.

The number of sites in the region has grown to be one of the largest in EGEE with 23 production EGEE sites spread over 8 countries**. The region supports over 15 Virtual Organizations with over 3300 CPU cores and 1500 TB of computing resources.

During EGEEII APROC has helped 12 sites deploy Grid middleware services and become certified production sites. This typically takes from 1-4 months of consulting and technical support to fully certify and deploy each site depending on the expertise and time available at each site.

To support sites in AsiaPacific, APROC has deployed and maintained 7 centralized Grid services at ASGC. These services provide the region with capabilities such as service discovery, job management, file management, transfer management, authorization, etc. ASGC has also developed High Availability system configuration for Information System services to increase the reliability of this service.

To quickly detect service faults in the region, APROC continuously monitor EGEE sites in the Asia Pacific region. ASGC uses centralized monitoring tools including GStat which is the primary Information System monitoring tool used by EGEE operations. GStat is developed and operated by ASGC. ASGC has also deployed regional tools monitoring tools to help quickly detect faults in the region such as Smokeping and Nagios. For Nagios, ASGC has also developed over 15 customized plugins to monitor Grid services.

Once problems are discovered, APROC notifies resource centers and provides expert technical support to help resolve issues. Support channels provided by ASGC to users and sites include email, telephone and ticketing system. From May 2006 to April 2008, ASGC has helped resolved 691 issued from the GGUS ticketing system.

During EGEE II, APROC has served as global operations support for 25 weeks, helping to monitor, coordinate and resolve issues for the global Grid infrastructure. ASGC has also served as first line user support for EGEE for 13 weeks, addressing users issues and identifying appropriate support staff for second line support.

Service availability for the region has improved from 60-70% in 2005 to 70-80% in 2008. Most failures were related to Data Management tests. These tests were found to be sensitive to the availability and performance of Information System components. Many of performance issues have been addressed by hardware upgrades and middleware improvements. One of the most important root causes of many failures is poor network performance and availability. Many problems were found to be related to congestion in both the WAN and LAN levels.

x509 certificates issued from IGTF Certificate Authorities are required to use and operate Grid services. To ensure that researchers can quickly participate in EGEE, ASGC runs a regional catch CA for EGEE and LCG collaborators in the Asia-Pacific region who do not have a domestic CA that can support them. ASGCCA currently has Registration Authorities (RA) in Taiwan, Korea, India, Malaysia,

New Zealand, Philippines and Vietnam. Many of these RA have been established to prepare for sites interested in joining EGEE.

EGEE infrastructure has continue to expand and improve in availability in the Asia Pacific region through the combined efforts of the EGEE central operations, APROC and the Grid sites in the region.

** Australia, China, India, Japan, Korea, Malaysia, Pakistan and Taiwan

3. EGEE III Asia-Pacific

The following section proposes some ideas on the direction and activities for EGEE III in Asia-Pacific Region.

The overall objective of EGEE Asia-Pacific (EAP) region will be to promote collaboration in E-Science and scientific research between Europe and Asia and within Asia itself. The results should be evaluated by the quality of number of collaborations established based on the extended EGEE infrastructure. To efficiently achieve results EAP should leverage the existing application communities and infrastructure created by EGEE. Developing regional communities that can gain real benefits from the infrastructure will create sustainability.

In addition EAP should directly benefit from the EGEE middleware development and integration effort. This will help reduce effort needed for interoperation related work. Interoperations will be too significant of a task in Asia-Pacific, since many countries have integrated their own middleware stack that is always in constantly changing.

Application

According to the country reports and requirements collected, high energy physics, biomedicine and earth science are of major interests for researchers in Asia Pacific. Apart from LHC experiment, many other high energy physics researches are making use of grid infrastructure and have alredy been integrated into EGEE infrastructure in this region, such as the Belle (Australia, Taiwan, and Japan), and CDF (Japan, Korea, and Taiwan). Biomedicine is still the e-Science application with the greatest general interest in Asia Pacific, drug discovery is the project undergoing in EGEE III, and proton therapy will be another new collaboration. Moreover, sea level changes, global earth observation, earthquake information system and disaster mitigation are of primary concern in Asia countries. EAP will foster the network of each application community and is targeting the three application areas first by integrating current applications and synergies.

Operations

EAP should extend operations technology and experience to partner countries. Operations in Asia-Pacific is currently centralized at APROC in Taiwan. However, it is possible to create a federated Regional Operations Center where tasks are distributed among EAP partners that can specialize in facets of operations.

By the time EGEE III begins, most countries should have established an EGEE resource center. EAP can then determine which partners have sufficient resources and help willing partners establish a national EGEE operation center. These centers will be responsible operations support for domestic resource centers.

For countries without a domestic Certification Authority (CA) that is approved by IGTF, APROC can continue to provide CA services. However, EAP should work with APGridPMA to assist partners to establish domestic CA to serve their local communities.

Training

Training in EAP will require EGEE to provide "training trainer" courses that will assist the region further develop it training capability and capacity. Specialize training targeted at select application communities and resource center administrators will also be required.

Networking

Networking in Asia-Pacific may be outside of the scope of EGEE, however it has large impact of Grid development in the region. There are a number of issues currently existing in this region:

- Relatively low bandwidth interconnecting countries in Asia-Pacific and to Europe.
- Disparate network projects do not transparently exchange routing with each other
- Usage-based charges for regional and international networks still exist and are discourage collaboration over the Internet.

Asia-Pacific network projects need to work together to develop high speed backbone and improve coverage in this region. An idea would be merge Asia-Pacific network projects to take advantage of each other strengths without duplicating effort. Effort should also be placed to address usage-based network charges and create an environment that will promote researchers and NRENs to use these networks.

4. Representative Summaries

Summary and overview of countries that were present during ISGC 2007. Slides can be obtained from: http://event.twgrid.org/isgc2007/program.htm#ISGC

◆ **Australia**

- **Representative**:Markus Buchhorn, Australian National University
- **NREN Status**:AARNet owns and operates a resilient and redundant multi-Gbps network across Australia. Diagrams of both domestic and international connectivity are shown in the diagrams below.

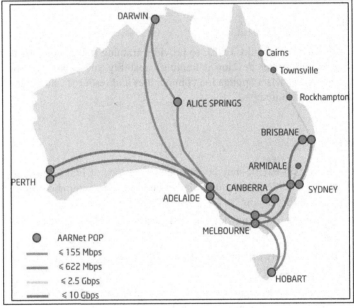

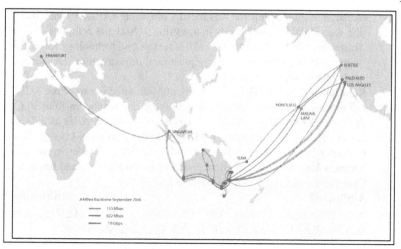

- **National Grid Initiative and Grid Activities Status**: National Collaborative Research Infrastructure Strategy (NCRIS) was introduced by Director Buchhorn. Through NCRIS, the Australian government is providing $542 million over 2005-2011 to provide researchers with major facilities, supporting infrastructure and networks necessary for world-class research. 12 specific priority capability areas have been identified: Evolving bio-molecular platforms and informatics, integrated biological systems, characterization, fabrication, biotechnology products, optical and radio astronomy, integrated marine capability, structure and evolution of the Australian continent, networked biosecurity framework, population health and clinical data linage, and terrestrial ecosystem research network. NCRIS will be implemented by the following platforms for collaboration:

(1). Australian national data service: building the Australian data commons and national registries and data sharing services to allow all researchers to deposit their data for re-use and preservation, within and across disciplines.

(2). National computational infrastructure: developing a shared national computational facility and domain oriented advanced modeling capabilities.

(3). Interoperability and collaboration infrastructure: developing services to link systems and resources nation wide and developing collaboration and workflow tools for researchers.

(4). Australian Research and Education Network: Connecting researchers and research resources at required bandwidth based on a shared authorization framework.

Australian Partnership for Advanced Computing (APAC) concluded in the second half of 2007 and is in transition to National computational infrastructure of NCRIS. NCRIS will leverage grid technology for the development and integration of computational infrastructure, data services and collaboration infrastructure.

- **Relationship with EGEE**: University of Melbourne is part of the NCRIS collaboration and has deployed and actively maintained an EGEE/LCG site since 2006. Their main focus has been to support Atlas as a Tier 2 center. However, University of Melbourne has also provided significant resources support for the biomed and belle VO. University of Melbourne's has extensive experience with gLite middleware and has held a Grid Administrator tutorial for KEK in late 2005.

- **Additional**   **Information**:
  http://event.twgrid.org/isgc2008/Presentation%20Meterial/Grid%20Activities%20in%20Asia%20Pacific/AP_Markus%20Buchhorn.pdf

◆ China

- **Representative**: Gang CHEN, Chinese Academy of Science
- **NREN Status**: Both CERNET and CSTNET deploy and operate domestic and international connectivity in China. Backbone links range from 2.5 to 10G connections. China has multiple international connections via APAN and TIEN2.

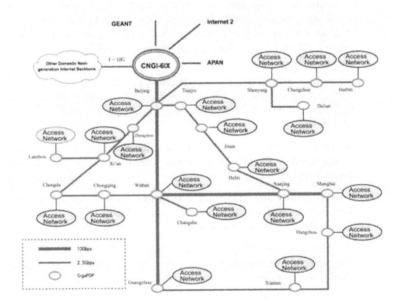

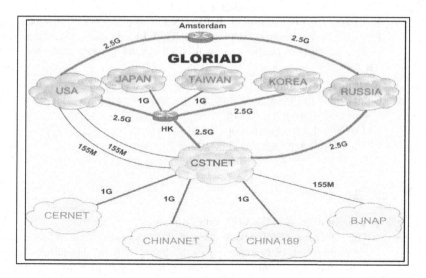

- **National Grid Initiative and Grid Activities Status**: Major Grid projects in China includes:

(1). China National Grid(CNGrid): supported by the national High-Tech R&D program, to develop a new information infrastructure, grid technology and grid applications. The HPC capability of CNGrid plans to reach 100 TFLOPS in 2008 and to achieve Petaflop level by 2010.

(2). China Education and Research Grid (ChinaGrid): funded by Ministry of Education for campus grid platform and applications of image processing, bioinformatics, computational fluid dynamics, and large scale information process.

(3). China Research and development environment Over Wide-area Network (CROWN): providing grid-enabled research environment for scientists, with pilot applications of bioinformatics, atmospheric sciences, scientific data grid and university digital museum, etc.

- **Relationship with EGEE**: EUChinaGrid initiative has allowed EGEE to establish close ties with China. EUChinaGrid is a 2 year 1.3 million Euro project starting January 2006. The project consists of 10 partners, 4 of which are from China. EUChinaGrid focuses on providing interoperability between EGEE and CNGRID, dissemination of Grid technology and strengthening scientific collaboration between Europe and China. Key application areas of EUChinaGrid includes:

    - High Energy Physics

    - Astrophysics

-        Bioinformatics

In additional to EUChinaGrid, IHEP, CNIC and more recently in 2008 Peking University have deployed LCG/EGEE production resource centers to enable collaboration with CMS, Atlas, Biomed and other experiments.

- **Additional Information:**
  ChinaGrid: http://www.chinagrid.edu.cn/
  CNGrid: http://www.cngrid.org/
  CROWN: http://www.crown.org.cn/en/
  EUChinaGrid: http://www.euchinagrid.org/

◆ India

- **Representative**: Atul GURTU, Tata Institute
- **NREN Status:** ERNET's backbone consist of both terrestrial and satellite with 14 Points of Presence across the contry. ERNET has also been able to establish a 45 Mbps connection to GEANT with plans to upgrade to 622 Mbps in 2007 and 1 Gbps in 2008.

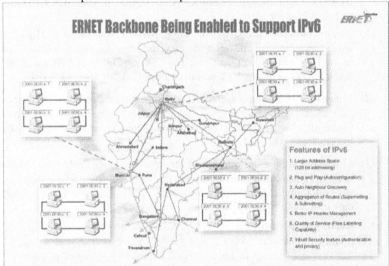

- **National Grid Initiative and Grid Activities Status:** Department of Information Technology (DIT), Govt. of India, has funded C-DAC (Centre for Development of Advanced Computing) to deploy nationwide computational Grid named GARUDA.

GARUDA connects 45 institutes in 17 cities across India over 10/100 Mbps network.

GARUDA middleware is based on GT2 while research will be performed on GT4 based middleware. Data management in GARUDA is based on Storage Resource Broker SRB.

GARUDA will focus on the following application communities:
- Computer Aided Engineering
- Earth Sciences
- High Energy Physics/Astro Physics
- Life Sciences
- Material Sciences / Nano Technology

- **Relationship with EGEE:** India has close relationship with EGEE via an associate project EUIndiaGrid which has a budget of 1.2 million EUR for a period of 2 years starting from Oct 2006. EUIndiaGrid is composed of 5 European and 9 Indian partners.
Key application areas of EUIndiaGrid includes:
- High Energy Physics
- Material Science
- Bioinformatics
- Earth and Atmospheric Science

In additional to EUInidiaGrid, TIFR and VECC have deployed Tier-2 LCG/EGEE resource centers to enable collaboration with CMS and Alice experiments.

Furthermore, interoperability between GARUDA and EGEE is undergoing for job submission from both sides. Grid information system interoperability is the key for job and resource information sharing. More collaborations are needed for the interoperation between the two systems.
- **Additional Information:** TIFR has a history of strong collaboration with CERN involving the development of computing fabric management tools, monitoring application and problem tracking systems. Many of these contributions are directly used within the EGEE project.
- http://www.ernet.in/index.htm
- http://www.euindiagrid.org/
- http://www.garudaindia.in/index.asp

◆ Indonesia

- **Representative:** Bobby Nazief, ITB

- **NREN Status:** Inherent (Indonesia Higher Education Research Network) is the first NREN in Indonesia, which connects almost 150 universities domestically, and TEIN2/3 is the primary gateway to the internet.

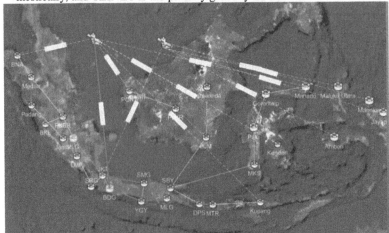

- **National Grid Initiative and Grid Activity Status:** InGrid is triggered by Inherent to build the grid facilities in Indonesia. Currently the focus is to build up the community, collect requirements of applications and develop the facilities. Interested grid applications includes bioinformatics, applied physics, applied chemistry, earth science, digital library, e-learning and earth observation.
- **Relationship with EGEE:** ITB is a partner of EUAsiaGrid which plans deploy gLite with the support of EGEE APROC.
- **Additional Information:**
- InGrid, http://grid.ui.ac.id/ingrid/pendaftaran

◆ Korea

- **Representative**: Beob Kyun KIM and Soonwook Hwang, KISTI
- **NREN Status**: KOREN (KOrea Advanced Research Network) operates the domestic research and education network in Korea. KOREN's domestic and international connectivity are shown below. It is also important to note that KOREN is connected to GLORIAD a ring network with 10G connecting Korea to Hong-Kong and the United States.

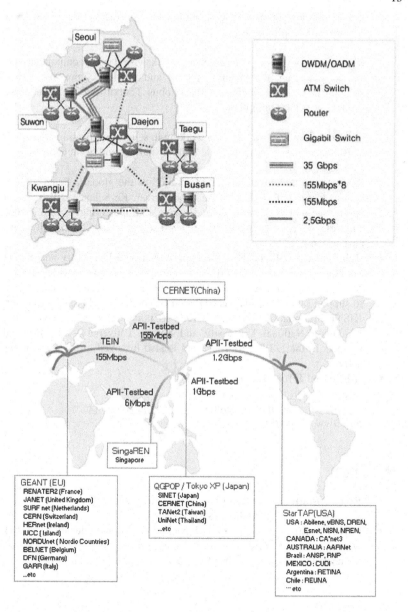

- **National Grid Initiative and Grid Activities Status**: K*Grid project is an initiative in Grid researches supported by MIC (Ministry of Information and Communication, Republic of Korea). The K*Grid project involves the development of Grid middleware, infrastructure and support for scientific applications.

K*Grid has developed a middleware stack with 3 core components: resource allocation, information systems and parallel computing. Each component extends features of the Globus Toolkit and all middleware services are OGSI compliant.

Researchers in K*Grid has been working in several application areas such as Biotechnology, Computational Fluid Dynamics and Nano technology.

Ke-Science was introduced in ISGC 2008 as the global e-Science gateway of Korea with KISTI as the major driver. Ke-Science will focus on applications of e-Physics, e-LifeScience, e-Engineering, e-GeoScience and Tele-Science by developing common software and collaboration support systems.

- **Relationship with EGEE**: Kyungpook National University and KISTI both have established EGEE/LCG resources centers and provides support for CMS and Alice (as Tier-2 center) experiments. There is also interest to support other VOs such as CDF and Biomed at KISTI resource center. KISTI in collaboration with CKCS (Chonnam National University, Kangnung National University and Sejong University) are unfunded partners in the EGEE II project and is also involved in SA1 operations activity.
- **Additional Information**:
- http://www.gridcenter.or.kr/index.htm
- http://www.jp.apan.net/meetings/0701-manila/Bykim.ppt
- http://www.koren21.net

◆ Japan

- **Representative:** Hiroyuki Matsunaga, University of Tokyo
  Takashi SASAKI, KEK
- **NREN Status:** Super SINET is Japan's research and education network with a backbone consisting of 10G connections. Japan is also directly connected to many of Asian's NRENs through the APAN network.

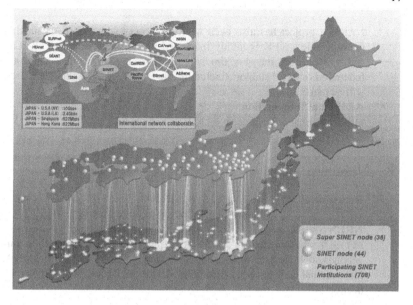

- **National Grid Initiative and Grid Activities Status**: NAREGI, Japan's National Research Grid Initiative, was created in 2003 by the Ministry of Education, Culture, Sports, Science and Technology (MEXT). NEREGI has developed Grid middleware for super-computers and computational clusters to support Japan's Cyber Science Infrastructure (CSI).

  NAREGI initially developed middleware components based on UNICORE and has more recently released middleware based on OGSA specification in May 2006.

  NAREGI has a strong focus in both bio and nano-technology applications.

- **Relationship with EGEE**: Japan and in particular University of Tokyo has a long history of working with European Data Grid (EDG) and was one of the earliest sites to join the LCG/EGEE production Grid in support of the Atlas experiment. University of Tokyo has also provided local training to Japanese Institutes for gLite User Interface installation and the usage of gLite and Atlas experiment software.

  KEK has also joined the EGEE infrastructure and have brought in new VOs such as Belle and Asia Pacific Data Grid. Support for other HEP and life science communities are also provided by KEK resource center in EGEE. KEK is also planning for expanded deployment of gLite with 5 collaborating institutes within Japan. KEK is also plans to hold EGEE system administration training in Japanese later this year.

NAREGI project has also been working closely with EGEE on making interoperable. KEK is highly interested in the interoperability of gLite and NAREGI. At the same time, the future strategy of the regional center federation on HEP support (including super B, T2K, ILC, and LHC etc.) will be made soon.

- **Additional Information**:
- http://www.naregi.org/index_e.html

◆ Malaysia

- **Representative:** Luke Jing YUAN, MIMOS
  Suhaimi Napis, Universiti Putra Malaysia, MYREN
- **NREN Status**:
  MYREN was launched in 2005 connecting 12 of the largest public universities in Malaysia, with bandwidths ranging from 2Mbps to 8Mbps. International connectivity is available via TIEN2 through a 45 Mbps connection.

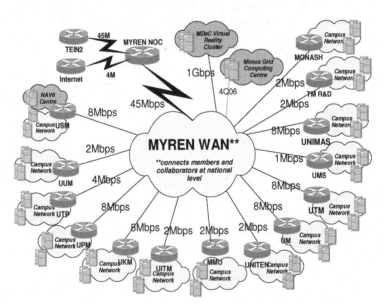

MYREN Network Topology (as of Aug 2006)

- **National Grid Initiative and Grid Activities Status:** The National Grid Computing Initiative (NGCI) is Malaysia's national Grid project lead by the Ministry of Science and Technology, Innovation (MOSTI).

The application domain areas in NGCI include the following:

- Scientific and engineering applications

- Humanities, Social Science and Find Arts

- E-Learning

- Life Sciences

The KnowledgeGrid Malaysia was introduced by Luke in ISGC 2008, which is a new initiative for national wealth and value creation via super computing power. Two of the major applications in KnowledgeGrid were also presented: eBioChem and eRender (support for Malaysia's animation industry).

- **Relationship with EGEE**: Universiti Putra Malaysia has expressed interest in establishing an EGEE resource center and MIMOS has done so earlier in 2008 following an EGEE tutorial held in December in Kuala Lumpur.
- **Additional Information**:
  KnowledgeGrid Malaysia: www.knowledgegrid.net.my/
  http://nucleus.mygridusbio.net.my/ganglia/

◆ Philippines

- **Representative:** Rey Vincent P. Babilonia, ASTI
  Rafael P. Saldana, Ateneo de Manila University
- **NREN Status:** Philippine Research and Government Information Network links academic, research and government institutions in the Philippines.

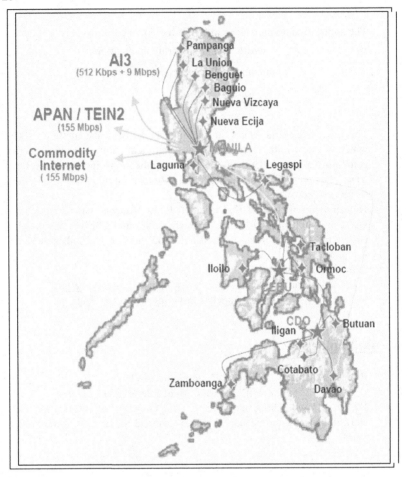

- **National Grid Initiative and Grid Activities Status**: The Philippine e-Science Grid Program is actively seeking to build a national Grid infrastructure, train people in relevant technologies and collaborate with the international Grid community.

Application areas that are higher priority are Bioinformatics (Agricultural and Medical) and Disaster Mitigation.
- **Relationship with EGEE**: APROC is currently working with Advanced Science and Technology Institute in deploying an EGEE Resource center.
- **Additional Information**:
  - http://www.asti.dost.gov.ph/

◆ Singapore

- **Representative:** Hing-Yan LEE , National Grid Office
- **NREN Status:** Singapore Advanced Research and Education Network (SingAREN) connects universities, research centers and similar non-profit institutes. Network connectivity for SingAREN is show below.

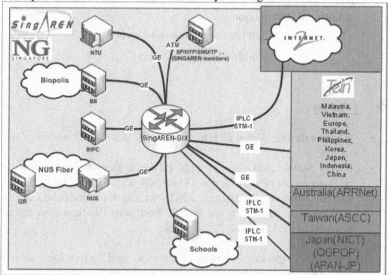

- **National Grid Initiative and Grid Activities Status:** The National Grid in Singapore started in November 2003 providing nearly 1000 CPU with some 15 Grid-enabled applications from the R&D community. The project is now in it's second phase and is co-funded by the two research councils of the A*STAR – Science & Engineering Research Council and Biomedical Research Council, the Defence Science & Technology Agency (DSTA), the Infocomm Development Authority (IDA) of Singapore, NUS and NTU.

National Grid employs a LSF-meta Scheduler to provide seamless access to distributed resources within the National Grid. The LSF-meta Scheduler is able to interface with local resource schedulers such as Sun's N1GE, LSF and PBS Pro.

Phase 2 of the National Grid focuses on promoting the adoption of Grid by industry and business users. Application areas of interest for the project include:

- digital media,

- collaborative manufacturing

- engineering services

- education

- **Relationship with EGEE:** The National Grid Office has deployed and operated an EGEE production site for more than 2 years. Singapore has contributed significant resources to both the EGEE HEP and biomed VOs during this period.
- **Additional Information:**

  - http://www.ngp.org.sg/index.html

  - http://www.singaren.net.sg/

◆ Taiwan

- **Representative**: Simon C. Lin, Academia Sinica Grid Computing Center (ASGC)
- **NREN Status:** ASGCNet extends Taiwan's international network connectivity to Asia-Pacific at speeds of 2.5Gbps for Japan and Hong-Kong and 622Mbps for Singapore. ASGCNet has also established the first 10Gbps direct link to Europe in 2007 from Asia Pacific region and also connects to the US with a 2.5Gbps link.

TWAREN operates domestic research and education network. TWAREN also provides connectivity to the US of 1.2 Gbps.

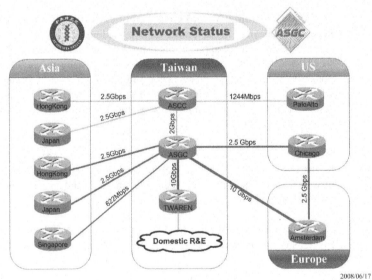

- **National Grid Initiative and Grid Activities Status:** TWGrid lead by Academia Sinica Grid Computing Center (ASGC) funded by the National Science Council include 7 partner institutes operating 8 resource centers. TWGrid has adopted the gLite middleware and is directly integrated into the EGEE production Grid. TWGrid also hosts an LCG Tier-1 center supporting Tier-2 centers in the region.

  TWGrid is involved with the following applications areas:

  - Bioinformatics
  - Earth Science
  - Digital Archive
  - High Energy Physics
  - Humanities and Social Science

- **Relationship with EGEE:** Taiwan has participated as one of the earliest resource center in LCG production Grid. The resource center is located at Academia Sinica and serves as a regional LHC Tier-1 center. This later led to the involvement into the EGEE Phase I, where Taiwan began operating as an EGEE Regional Operation Center in April of 2004. Taiwan has helped the region to grow to one of the largest region in EGEE. Taiwan has also participated in Wisdom project and has played a key role in the Avian Flu Data Challenge. Continuing in EGEE phase II, ASGC participates as a partner in NA2, NA3, NA4 and SA1. Since 2004 Taiwan has provided 12 tutorials domestically and 6 in Asia Pacific (Beijing, Mumbai, Manila, Singapore, Vietnam and Kuala Lumpur).

- **Additional Information:**

  - http://www.twgrid.org/

◆ Thailand

- **Representative:** Piyawut Srichaikul, NECTEC
  Royal Chitradon, Hydro and Agro Informatics Institute, National Science and Technology Development Agency Ministry of Science and Technology

- **NREN Status:** In 2006 the inter-university network UNINET and Thai research network ThaiSARN are combined together to form the Thai Research and Education Network ThaiREN.

  UNINET connects over 130 research and education institutes in Thailand. The network provides the service speed of 155 Mbps to 2.5 Gbps in Bangkok and 34-155 Mbps elsewhere.

- **National Grid Initiative and Grid Activities Status:** The Thai National Grid Project is a national project under Software Industry Promotion Agency, Ministry of Information and Communication Technology. The project is operated by the Thai National Grid Center. The project has expanded from 14 member institutes to 21 organizations in 2007 and collaborates with industry and international partners such as PRAGMA, AIST and SDSC.

  ThaiGrid will has the following 5 initial focus areas:
  - Life Science
    - o Drug Design
  - Computational Science and Engineering
    - o Geoinformatics, CFD
  - Digital media
    - o Rendering
  - Enterprise computing
    - o WS/SOA Enterprise computing application
    - o Industrial Simulation and Modeling
    - o Financial analysis
  - Education

- o   E-learning, collaborative environment

- o   Grid education

At this stage, ThaiGrid is moving from infrastructure to services and wider application domains.

- **Relationship with EGEE**: National Electronics and Computer Technology Center NECTEC has expressed interest in working with gLite middleware.
- **Additional Information:**
  - THaiGrid, http://www.thaigrid.or.th

  - http://iir.ngi.nectec.or.th/internet/map/firstpage.html

◆ Vietnam

- **Representative:** Tran Van Lang, Do Van Long, HCM City Institute of Information Technology
- **NREN Status:** Vietnam Research and Education Network (VinaREN) consist of a backbone that connects 5 major network operation centers in Vietnam. There are also plans to extend this network to connect over 50 institutions. International connectivity is also available through TIEN2 through a 45Mbps link.

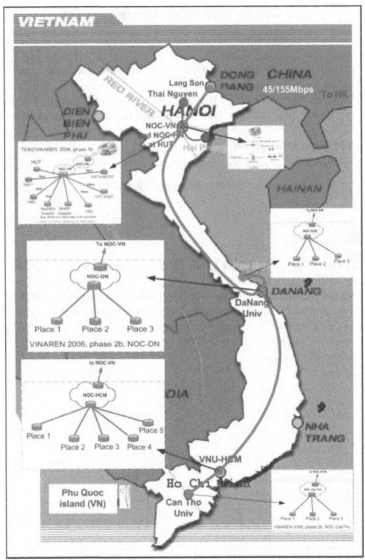

- **National Grid Initiative and Grid Activities Status**: VNGrid Project is financed by the Ministry of Science and Technology of Vietnam and is a two year project that will end in Oct 2008 with a budge of 160 thousand USD. The project aims to build a Grid infrastructure to connect five institutes in Vietnam and achieve interoperation with other Grid systems.

VNGrid aims to build applications in the following areas
- Bioinframatics

- Meterology
- Virtual Reality
- Cryptography
- Collaborative environments

• **Relationship with EGEE**:
  HCM City Institute of Information Technology has expressed interest in working with gLite middleware.

• **Additional Information**:

  - http://www.tein2.net/upload/pdf/TEIN2-VN-VinaREN-APEC2006dante.pdf

  - http://www.ioit-hcm.ac.vn

Grid Operation at Tokyo Tier-2 Centre for ATLAS

Hiroyuki Matsunaga, Tadaaki Isobe, Tetsuro Mashimo, Hiroshi Sakamoto & Ikuo Ueda

International Centre for Elementary Particle Physics, the University of Tokyo, Japan

Abstract

International Centre for Elementary Particle Physics, the University of Tokyo, has been involved in the Worldwide LHC Computing Grid since 2003. After extensive R&D experience of the PC computing farm, disk and tape storage systems, network technology and the integration of these components, it is now operating a regional centre for the ATLAS data analysis. The regional centre includes an ATLAS Tier-2 site which is running the gLite middleware developed by the Enabling Grids for E-sciencE (EGEE) project. One of the biggest challenges at the regional centre is efficient data transfer between the Tier-2 site in Tokyo and other sites, in particular the associated Tier-1 site in France, because the large round trip time due to the long distance makes it difficult to transfer data at a high rate. We have been studying to achieve a good performance of the data transfer, and some results of network tests and ATLAS data transfer are described. Hardware and software components and the operational experience are also reported in this article.

1. Introduction

International Centre for Elementary Particle Physics (ICEPP), the University of Tokyo was established originally in 1974, aiming at studying the most fundamental particles and forces of nature experimentally by using the world's most for front accelerators. In the past, ICEPP has been involved in several collider experiments at DESY and CERN in Europe, and now the main project is the ATLAS experiment at the Large Hadron Collider (LHC). The LHC is the world largest accelerator which has been constructed at CERN near Geneva and is almost ready to start operations. The first collision will be expected in 2008.

At the LHC, data volume coming from the detector becomes huge due to the high-energy and high-luminosity proton beams and a huge number of readout channels of the detectors. The amount of data produced at the LHC experiments will be 15PB per year, and the processing power will require more than 10 million Spe-

S.C. Lin and E. Yen (eds.), *Production Grids in Asia: Applications, Developments and Global Ties*, DOI 10.1007/978-1-4419-0046-3_2,
© Springer Science + Business Media, LLC 2010

cInt 2000 (SI2000). Consequently the experiments require very large data storage capacity, very high data processing speed and very wide data transfer bandwidth. As a result, even CERN, the world largest accelerator laboratory, can't afford to provide the necessary computing resources for the data analysis. On the other hand, the LHC experiment collaborations have been very large and international, and recent development of the Wide-Area Network (WAN) connectivity enabled distributed data analysis by connecting computing centres of the collaborating institutes around the world. The LHC experiments decided to utilize the Grid technology for the distributed computing framework to analyze their data. The Worldwide LHC Computing Grid (WLCG) was created to enable the data analysis for LHC experiments with the Grid. It is an international collaboration of the physics laboratories and institutes which contribute resources, the four LHC experiments (ALICE, ATLAS, CMS, LHCb), and the Grid projects providing software (EGEE, OSG and Nordugrid).

In Japan, it was decided that ICEPP should operate a regional centre for ATLAS at the University of Tokyo to enable efficient data analysis by the Japanese collaborators. At present ICEPP is running a Tier-2 Grid site (named TOKYO-LCG2) as a member of the WLCG collaboration, and is also providing a local analysis facility for the Japanese collaborators in ATLAS. The Tier-2 site has been involved in the WLCG and ATLAS distributed computing activities for the last few years. Overview of the regional centre and the recent operational experience will be shown below.

2. Hardware

We, at ICEPP, have been studying on the computer fabric and the site operation by using the pilot systems since 2002[1]. In this study, PC farms, disk storages, tape drives and network devices were tested extensively, and expertise of the Grid deployment has been acquired. Based on this study the production system for the regional centre was procured by international tendering in 2006, and started running from January 2007.

The production system (Fig. 1) has been placed in the new computer room (_270m2) dedicated to the regional centre. Electric power is supplied through uninterruptible power supplies (UPS) to all computing components as well as air conditioners. Under a room space constraint, blade server is used in the PC farm (Grid worker nodes and local batch nodes) and Grid head nodes thanks to the high density and low power consumption. We introduced Dell PowerEdge 1955, with dual Xeon 3160 CPUs (WoodCrest 3.0GHz, dual core), 4 or 8GB memory (2GB/core is necessary for the ATLAS reconstruction program) and 73GB local Serial Attached SCSI (SAS) disk drives in a mirroring (RAID-1) configuration by hardware RAID. There are 650 blade nodes in total.

As for the data storage, an external RAID system (Infortrend EonStor A16FG2422) was chosen based on good performance experience in the pilot system, as a cost-effective solution in order to have as much disk space as possible. It contains 16 Serial ATA (SATA) hard disk drives (500GB each) and has a 4Gb Fibre Channel host interface. The disk storage can be accessed through a disk server (Dell PowerEdge 2950, 8GB memory) which is equipped with a 10GbE network interface card (Chelsio T210-SR) for the network connection and a 4Gb Fibre Channel host bus adapter (QLogic QLE2462). Both the RAID systems and the disk servers are connected to Fibre Channel switches (QLogic SANbox 5600). Each disk server serves 5 filesystems (35TB in total), each of which is provided from the RAID system configured as one RAID-6 partition. We have 140 RAID systems which correspond approximately to 1PB.

Sun StorageTek SL8500 is our tape library system. In the present configuration, it has 8000 tape slots and 32 tape drives, and LTO 3 tape cartridges (400GB capacity) are used. Each tape drive are connected to a tape server (Dell PowerEdge 1950) with a 2Gb Fibre Channel host bus adapter (QLogic QLA2342-CK). This system is currently setting up as a component of a hierarchical storage management (HSM) system, and will be used at the local facility in the near future.

There are four Ethernet switches (three Foundry RX-16's and one RX-4) for the data transmission in the regional centre. For connections with the blade servers, we use 1000Base-T high-density line cards with mini RJ-21 interfaces to reduce number of cables.

ICEPP signed the WLCG Memorandum of Understanding (MoU), in which we pledged to provide 1000kSI2000 of CPU, 200TB of disk and 2000Mbps of WAN connection in 2007. In 2008 additional 200TB of disk is pledged to provide and it is now in preparation. The next major hardware upgrade will be done by 2010 at ICEPP, and the pledged numbers in the MoU would change in future according to the actual ATLAS activity and the next procurement result.

Fig. 1 Picture of the computer room. The blade servers and the RAID systems are mounted in the racks. A tape library system is placed at the far side.

3. Software

At our regional centre, a part of resources is provided to the Tier-2 Grid site and the rest (local facility) is used by the Japanese collaborators only. These two parts are logically separated and we manage these two in different ways, except for Operating System (OS) installation and fabric monitoring. The local facility can be accessed even without the Grid software, and we will provide local users with data accesses to the data storages between the two domains.

3.1 Grid middleware

The gLite middleware developed by EGEE is used at the Tier-2 site. The gLite 3.0 has been installed on Scientific Linux CERN 3 (SLC3) OS with 32bit architecture on all nodes but Worker Nodes (WNs) and Storage Element (SE) nodes.

On the WNs, gLite 3.1 has been installed on SLC4 32bit OS since 2007 as it was requested from the ATLAS. As for the SE, the Disk Pool Manager (DPM) ha been deployed since it is recommended to use at a Tier-2 site (not having a tape storage) and it is relatively easy to operate. We have one head node and six disk servers for the SE. On the head node, several important services (srmv1, srmv2, srmv2.2, dpm, dpns and MySQL as a backend database) are running, while actual data transfer is performed on the disk server on which a GridFTP daemon is running. The disk server has gLite 3.0 installed on SLC4 x86 64 OS because the OS allows us to make a 6 TB filesystem on a RAID partition and Linux kernel 2.6 in SLC4 should be better than kernel 2.4 in SLC3. For the filesystem of the DPM disk pool, we introduced XFS (by SGI) which handles large files better and is faster in deleting a large amount of data files than ext3, which is the default file system in recent Linux distributions. Also, XFS requires 64bit OS due to its implementation. In the burn-in tests before the deployment, we found that XFS in the SLC4 was not stable enough in case a filesystem was almost full; hence we had to modify some kernel parameters to avoid a kernel crash. The DPM recently implemented the Storage Resource Manager (SRM) v2.2 protocol, and this has been configured with the space tokens at ICEPP as requested by ATLAS.

As the local batch system in Computing Element (CE), we are using Torque and-Maui included in the gLite middleware. We have no major problem with 480 CPU cores in 120 WNs, but if we want to provide more CPU cores and/or WNs we may migrate to LSF (Load Sharing Facility) of Platform that is already in use at the local facility.

In addition to the above-mentioned services, we have top-level and site BDIIs, MON, RB (Resource Broker) and MyProxy, LFC (LCG File Catalogue) with MySQL backend, and UI (User Interface) nodes in production at our site.

We have a testbed for the gLite middleware deployment. The middleware upgrade sometimes requires a configuration change and the gLite middleware itself as well as its configuration tool (YAIM) have often bugs. We usually try to upgrade the middleware on the testbed before doing this on the production system in order to validate it. It is very useful to avoid instability or an unnecessary downtime.

3.2   Other softwares and tools

For the local analysis facility, we have different strategy than the Tier-2 Grid site. Since its computing resource is larger than that of the Tier-2 site and data access pattern is different, performance and functionality are sometimes more important than stability.

In the CPU farm in the local facility, we are using LSF as the batch system, although Torque/Maui was mainly used in the past pilot systems and is also used at our Tier-2 site even now. The reason is that numbers of CPU cores are so many that we have not tried with Torque/Maui, and Torque/Maui does not provide sufficient functionalities for fine-grained configuration. We have been running LSF for more than a year, and we would like to deploy it in the Tier-2 site as well in the future.

The local disk storage can be accessed by NFS (Network File System) version 3 at present since we have had good experience with it and many users like having access to a filesystem instead of using a special IO protocol. However, as data volume becomes large we want to integrate the tape system in our storage system by using CASTOR (CERN Advanced Storage Manager) version 2, a HSM system developed by CERN. We carried out some tests with CASTOR 1 with the pilot system, and are currently setting up CASTOR 2 in the production system. After the functional tests we will start using CASTOR 2 soon, and perhaps will replace DPM with CASTOR 2 at the Tier-2 site in future.

A key component of the CASTOR is the Oracle relational database. In the production system of the regional centre, we set up Oracle 10g with 2-node RAC (Real Application Clusters) configuration. It is to be used with CASTOR and the gLite middleware, and possibly for ATLAS conditions databases by replicating from another Tier-1 site. We are still getting experience of Oracle with the FTS (File Transfer Service) in gLite.

We provide 10 interactive nodes at the local facility. To allow for balancing loads, round robin DNS is used for them. They also act as gLite UI nodes and submission nodes to the LSF batch system. Users' home directories and ATLAS software are served by NFS, but we are trying to migrate to AFS (Andrew File System) that should have better scalability with a cache on the client side and a read-only replication on the server side. The deployment of AFS has been almost done, but the integration with LSF is still in progress.

We set up Quattor (developed by CERN) servers to install OS on most nodes and to manage rpm packages and configuration files on the local facility node. At the Tier-2 site, apt/yum and YAIM are used for package upgrade and gLite configuration, respectively. We prepared Quattor templates by ourselves. The OS installation by Quattor is performed through the PXE (Preboot eXecution Environment).

3.3   Monitor programs

For monitoring purposes, we are using several programs from fabric to Grid services. Some are provided by the vendors and some are made by us. We describe these softwares below.

Lemon (LHC Era Monitoring) is a server/client monitoring system. A sensor is running on each client node and a server collects monitoring information from the clients and visualizes the data through web interface. Because we do not use Oracle as the backend database, an alarm function does not work. To enable alarm, we are going to deploy Nagios which is widely used even in the Grid community.

MRTG (Multi Router Traffic Grapher) and Smokeping are tools for monitoring network statistics and latency/connectivity, respectively. Both programs use RRDtool (Round Robin Database Tool) internally to store and graph data. MRTG gets statistics data of each port of the Ethernet switches with SNMP (Simple Network Management Protocol). Smokeping is to measure a round trip time (RTT) to designated node or router.

We installed Dell OpenManage on all Dell servers. It checks hardware status and logs events. With IT Assistant from Dell, one can see all events from the web browser. Infortrend provides the RAIDWatch Manager to manage their RAID systems. We can get emails from the RAIDWatch notifying a failure of a hard disk drive or a RAID controller.

The gLite middleware does not provide monitoring tools enough to check the Grid services. Some monitoring information is provided by GStat (using the BDII data) and GridICE (Lemon-like sensor), and the APROC (Asia-Pacific Regional Operations Centre), which supports TOKYO-LCG2 operations, monitors Grid services and network status of our site, but they are still not sufficient for us. We have created some tools to monitor the DPM. The first one is to calculate data transfer rates of the GridFTP servers. It parses GridFTP logs on the disk servers and makes graphs of the data transfer rates per domain name, such as cern.ch. Although it is not very accurate (each log message has only start and end times of a transfer and thus the only average rate can be calculated, and an aborted transfer is not logged), this is very useful, together with the MRTG information of the disk servers. Another home-made tool makes a disk usage table of the DPM. A Perl script runs once a day to retrieve information directly from the MySQL backend database. One can check the disk usage in a directory or owned by a user/group with a web browser.

4. Network and Data Transfer

4.1 Network

Network connectivity with other Grid sites is crucial issue, especially at the ICEPP Tier-2 site. In the ATLAS computing model a Tier-2 site must be associated with one Tier-1 site, and the Tier-2's activities (data transfer and job submission) should be mostly limited to that with the associated Tier-1. In our case, it is CC-IN2P3 (Lyon, France) which is very far from Japan and the RTT between the two sites is 280ms.

ASGC (Taipei, Taiwan) is an additional Tier-1 candidate for ICEPP because it is the nearest ATLAS Tier-1 site (RTT is 30ms) and they help Grid operations of our site as the Regional Operation Centre (ROC), as mentioned above. However, the network link between Tokyo and Taipei (maintained by ASGC) had only 622Mbps bandwidth until last year. It is currently 1Gbps and will be upgraded to 2.4Gbps in the near future. We performed some network and data transfer tests between ASGC and ICEPP, but we have not had formal ATLAS activity with ASGC yet.

In Japan, SINET (Science Information Network) is the major National Research and Education Network (NREN). The bandwidth is 10 to 40Gbps at the backbone, and most ATLAS collaborating institutes in Japan connect to SINET with 1Gbps or more. The ICEPP regional centre connects to SINET with 10Gbps, through the University router. In order not to reduce the available bandwidth, we do not use any IDS or Firewall, but apply an access control list (ACL) at the switches.

SINET provides an international link to New York, where GEANT (European academic network) is also connected. GEANT connects to RENATER (French NREN) to which the CC-IN2P3 connects. Although SINET, GEANT and RENATER are all public lines shared with other traffic, the bandwidth is 10Gbps all the way from ICEPP to CC-IN2P3 since February 2008. Before then, it was limited to 2.4Gbps at the connection between SINET and GEANT routers at New York.

4.2   Data Transfer

It is well known that it is difficult to achieve high performance with TCP over long distance wide-bandwidth network (so-called Long Fat pipe Network, LFN). In TCP, congestion control is realized by changing a window size. Since data transfer rate is roughly given by window size / RTT, the congestion control is critical in order to have high transfer rate. Network condition is also important, because once a packet is lost then TCP window size shrinks and long time is required to recover. This recovering behaviour depends on the TCP implementation. In Linux kernel 2.6 (SLC4) the default TCP implementation is BIC TCP which behaves better than TCP Reno in kernel 2.4 (SLC3) for the congestion control. This is another reason why SLC4 is used on the DPM disk servers.

Another way to improve data transfer rate is to increase number of data streams. In gLite or other Grid middlewares, GridFTP is a standard program used for widearea file transfer. It makes TCP connections in parallel to send a file in multiple streams. Moreover, we can run multiple GridFTP programs concurrently to send multiple files. In the WLCG, data transfer using GridFTP is controlled by a software called File Transfer Service (FTS) in gLite. With FTS, one can set a channel between two SEs, like IN2P3-TOKYO, and set numbers of data streams and concurrent files for a channel. In ATLAS, FTS is usually used from the Distributed Data Management (DDM) system called Don Quijote2 (DQ2) [2].

We set the TCP parameters (window sizes and so on) of the Linux kernel on the disk servers to modest values (up to 4MB) by using YAIM, but increased number of data streams and number of concurrent file transfers to 10 and 20, respectively, in FTS. These settings have not been fine-tuned but give reasonably good results for data transfer between CC-IN2P3 and ICEPP, without memory exhaustion on the disk servers thanks to many disk servers at both sites.

In order to check network condition, TCP performance was measured with iperf-program between test machines set up at both sites. All the test machines have 1GbE network interface card, hence it is impossible to test 10Gbps WAN bandwidth but still useful to detect unusual condition. TCP window size was able to grow up to 8MB. As a first step, we confirmed that 32bit SLC3 gave worse performance than 32bit SLC4, thus we decided to use 32bit SLC4 boxes afterward. Fig. 2 shows measurement results of iperf in both directions for about 9 days. Numbers of parallel streams was set to 1, 2, 4 and 8 in iperf. From CC-IN2P3 to ICEPP, transfer rates nearly reached the 1Gbps limit of the NIC with 8 streams most of the time, while in the opposite direction it was much worse and unstable. We have not yet understood the reason of the difference, but we are not worried about this asymmetry very much because data transferred from Tier-1 to Tier-2 would be much larger than that from Tier-2 to Tier-1; the former deals with real detector data, but the latter doesn't. However, we hope that the recent network upgrade at New York (2.4Gbps to 10Gbps) has improved performance.

Data transfers in ATLAS has been going on for a long time by using Monte Carlo simulation data or cosmic ray data. In most cases, the ICEPP Tier-2 site receives data from the CC-IN2P3 Tier-1 site. Fig. 3 shows a snapshot of data traffic to the disk servers at ICEPP during a cosmic run in March 2008. It was created by our own monitor program mentioned in 3.3. There were 6 disk servers used at ICEPP and more than 30 disk servers (Solaris, ZFS filesystem) at CC-IN2P3. During the transfer, a peak rate of 140MB/s was observed when both FTS and DQ2 were in good shape.

When we will add 200TB of disk storage (and disk servers) to the Tier-2 site soon, we will also upgrade gLite middleware from 3.0 (32bit) to 3.1 (64bit) on the DPM nodes. GridFTP in gLite 3.1 has been upgraded to version 2 which enhances performance very much. After these upgrades, performance of the data transfer should be improved further.

38

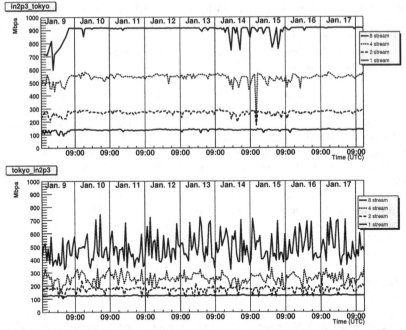

Fig. 2 Network throughputs were measured with iperf program from January 9 to January 17, 2008. Top figure is for CC-IN2P3 to ICEPP, and bottom is for ICEPP to CC-IN2P3. 1Gbps was the absolute maximum of the bandwidth limited at the 1GbE NIC at the both test nodes. We observed bad performance in ICEPP-to-CC-IN2P3 case, but the reason is not understood.

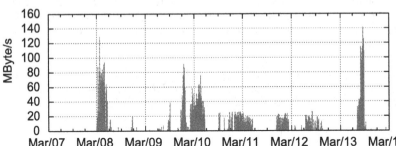

Fig. 3 Data transfer rate from CC-IN2P3 to ICEPP during a cosmic run in March 2008. This graph is created from GridFTP logs at the disk servers. A peak rate of 140MB/s was observed.

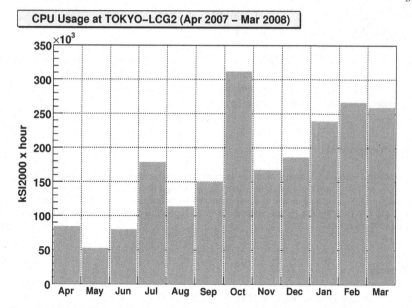

Fig. 4 Monthly CPU usage (in kSI2000_hour) at the ICEPP Tier-2 site from April 2007 to March 2008. Since most jobs are ATLAS Monte Carlo simulations, the usage variation over time depends on the ATLAS activity, although increasing tendency is observed.

5. CPU Usage

CPUs at the Tier-2 site has been used mostly by the ATLAS Monte Carlo simulation. In the last 12 months, from April 2007 to March 2008, 2.09×10^6 (kSI2000×hour) of CPU was used at the ICEPP Tier-2 site. This number is one of the largest contributions to the ATLAS experiment among Tier-2 sites. The usage had increasing tendency as shown in Fig. 4, and it could be increased further as there are still free batch slots from time to time and input data distribution for the Monte Carlo simulation jobs from CC-IN2P3 to ICEPP could be faster in future.

6. Summary

A regional centre for the ATLAS data analysis has been set up at ICEPP, the University of Tokyo. It is comprised of the Tier-2 Grid site and the local facility. Operations of the Tier-2 site have been stable, and availability and reliability measured by WLCG was over 90% recently, with help of monitor programs and use of a testbed. Within the ATLAS activity, data files are transferred from the associated Tier-1 site in France, and the Monte Carlo simulation jobs run on the PC farms constantly. A peak rate of 140MB/s was achieved recently for the data transfer, and we try to improve the rate further.

The regional centre is operated by 4_5 FTEs. Two system engineers from a company work with the ICEPP staff, mainly on the fabric, and the Tier-2 site is operated by ~1 FTE. This situation will be better once deployment of the new software is completed and the system becomes mature.

Acknowledgements

We would like to thank National Institute of Informatics (NII), network management team of the University of Tokyo, and Computing Research Centre of High Energy Accelerator Research Organization (KEK) for setting up and managing the network infrastructure. We are also grateful to ASGC and CC-IN2P3 staffs for their cooperation and support in performing network tests and data transfer operations.

References

[1]   M. Ishino et al., Nucl. Instr. Meth. A 534, 70 (2004).
[2]   M. Branco et al., J. Phys. Conference Series 119, 062017 (2008).

The EUAsiaGrid Project

Marco Paganoni

University of Milano-Bicocca and INFN, Italy

Abstract

The EUAsiaGrid proposal contributes to the aims of the Research Infrastructures part of the EU Seventh Framework Programme (FP7) by promoting interoperation between the European and the Asian-Pacific Grids. The project, with a total number of 15 partners coordinated by INFN, started on April 1st 2008. It will disseminate the knowledge about the EGEE Grid infrastructure, organize specific training events and support applications both within the scientific communities with an already long experience in the Computing Grids (High Energy Physics, Computational Chemistry, Bioinformatics and Biomedics) and in the most recent ones (Social Sciences, Disaster Mitigation, Cultural Heritage). Ultimately the EUAsiaGrid project will pave the way towards a common e-Infrastructure with the European and the Asian Grids.

1. Objectives

The EUAsiaGrid project aims to provide specific support actions to foster the integration of the Grid infrastructures between Europe and the Asia-Pacific region for the benefit of the many diverse scientific communities that have active partners in both continents. EUAsiaGrid will act as a support action, aiming to define and implement a policy to promote the gLite middleware developed within the EU EGEE project [1] across Asian countries. The dissemination in Asia of the knowledge about EGEE infrastructure, middleware and services aims to attract those research and education communities that require the analysis of large quantities of data, need huge amounts of computing power, or are looking for tight international collaborations to utilise shared resources. Training of these communities and support for their applications will allow them to make use of a much larger pool of storage and compute resources than currently available in non-Grid environments. EUAsiaGrid main actions will be to spread dissemination, provide training, support scientific applications and monitor the results. These activities will take place in synergy with the other Grid initiatives in Asia, namely EGEE-III via its Asia Federation, and both EUChinaGRID and EU-IndiaGRID.

The roadmap to reach the mentioned objectives can be outlined as follows:

S.C. Lin and E. Yen (eds.), *Production Grids in Asia: Applications, Developments and Global Ties*, DOI 10.1007/978-1-4419-0046-3_3,
© Springer Science + Business Media, LLC 2010

1.1 Promote awareness in the Asian countries of the EGEE infrastructures, middleware and services by means of public events and written and multi-media material.

1.2 Capture local e-Science user requirements in terms of resources needed, Grid services, application software, and training needs.

1.3 Identify and engage scientific communities that can benefit from the use of state-of-art Grid technologies.

1.4 Provide training resources and organize training events for potential and actual Grid users.

1.5 Support the scientific applications and create a human network of scientific communities by building on and leveraging the e-Science Grid infrastructure.

2. *Partners*

The EUAsiaGrid project partners, listed in Table 1, come mainly from the Asia-Pacific region. INFN, profiting from the long experience in Grid operations, dissemination and training is the coordinator partner. ASGC plays an essential role, leveraging on his role of ROC in the Asia Pacific region for the EGEE infrastructure.

Table1. EUAsiaGrid project partners

Beneficiary Name	Country
Istituto Nazionale di Fisica Nucleare	Italy
CESNET	Czech Republic
University of Manchester	UK
HealthGrid	France
School of Science and Engineering, Ateneo de Manila University	Philippines
Australia National University	Australia
Academia Sinica Grid Computing	Taiwan
Advanced Science and Technology Institute	Philippines
Hydro and Agro Informatics Institute	Thailand
Infocomm Development Authority	Singapore

Institute of Information Technology	Vietnam
Institut Teknologi Bandung	Indonesia
National Electronics and Computer Technology Centre	Thailand
Universiti Putra Malaysia	Malaysia
MIMOS Berhad	Malaysia

3. Scientific applications

The main applications that are being supported on the EGEE infrastructure by the EUAsiaGrid project are coming from the following scientific domains:

3.1. High Energy Physics:

During the LHC data taking several PB/year have to be analyzed by a worldwide spread community, gathered in two general purpose experiments, ATLAS and CMS. Both experiments use already gridified applications to produce simulated data, reconstruct and analyze the recorded data. ASGC and INFN participate with T1 centres for both ATLAS and CMS.

3.2 Computational chemistry:

Quite a few popular chemical software packages, both open source and commercial, are being gridified to use the gLite middleware [2]. CESNET has a long experience in the field.

3.3 Mitigation of natural disasters:

Asia Pacific is a hazard prone area, as many countries in this region are at relatively high risk of earthquakes, volcanoes, landslides, floods, droughts, and cyclones. Current effective disaster monitoring, mitigation, warning systems, and management systems are being re-viewed to be integrated with regional gLite based infrastructure, and to construct the content standards for hazard mitigation information systems.

3.4 Biomedics and Bioinformatics:

Genomics sequencing projects and new technologies applied to molecular genetics analysis as well as medical re-search and healthcare applications are producing huge amounts of raw data. The use of the Grid Computing has proved to be useful in relevant projects, for instance to speed-up the drug discovery process against neglected and emergent diseases such as Malaria and Avian Flu. HealthGrid has a long experience in the field.

3.5 Social Sciences:

Mathematical modelling is being used as a mean to address the grand challenges associated with problems such as globalisation, inter-national migration and uneven development. The use of a global Grid infrastructure, like EGEE enhances both the geographic reach and the computational power of these projects. The NCeSS unit at the University of Manchester is being involved since long time in these projects.

3.6 Digital cultural and heritage:

Digitization, modelling and visualization required in many areas of the digital culture and heritage have needs of Grid-enabled high performance computing power.

4. Dissemination and training

A web site http://www.euasiagrid.eu and wiki pages for each workpackage has been setup not only to allow easy communication within the project, but also to disseminate the interest in the EGEE infrastructure in the Asia Pacific region. Furthermore EUAsiaGrid is participating to a large number of national and international workshops and conferences with stands, dissemination materials, posters and oral presentation to reach a wide audience.

While dissemination provides a general picture of the project, training provides de-tailed technical information to the potential users and gives them the skills to use the Grid computing infrastructure allowing them to learn and practice. The targets of the training events are:

4.1 Technical personnel, to enable them to manage the e-Infrastructure and the user applications by using the Grid tools effectively;

4.2 Users of the scientific applications, to foster the use of the Grid e-Infrastructure by the scientific communities in the Asian countries.

The GILDA t-infrastructure [3], developed by INFN, is the main tool used for training. Training events will be collocated with already scheduled conferences and work-shop, in order to reduce the travel costs. Effective results are foreseen by making use of the "train the trainers" approach.

Both dissemination and training activities have to cope with large cultural and linguistic diversities as well as very different levels of engagement in the Grid activities in the different countries within the Asia Pacific region.

5.   Conclusions

Taking advantage of the EGEE Grid e-Infrastructure, the EUAsiaGrid project will encourage federating approaches across scientific disciplines and communities by means of resource sharing and cooperative work among researchers in Europe and in the Asia Pacific region.

References

[1]   http://public.eu-egee.org/
[2]   http://glite.web.cern.ch/glite/
[3]   https://gilda.ct.infn.it/

Part II Application – High Energy Physics, Biomedicine and Life Sciences, Humanities & Social Science

The e-Science for High Energy Physics in Korea

Kihyeon Cho and Hyunwoo Kim

e-Science Applications Research and Development Team

Korea Institute of Science and Technology Information (KISTI), Korea

Abstract

In this paper, we report the experiences and results of the integration and utilization of e-Science for high-energy physics in Korea. The e-Science for high-energy physics is to study high-energy physics any time and anywhere even if we are not on-site of accelerator laboratories. The contents are 1) data production, 2) data processing and 3) data analysis anytime and anywhere. The data production is to do remote control and take shifts remotely. The data processing is to run jobs anytime, anywhere using grid farms. The data analysis is to work together to publish papers using collaborative environment such as EVO (Enabling Virtual Organization) system. We apply this concept to high energy physics experiments, especially, ALICE experiment at CERN in Europe and CDF experiment at Fermi-lab. And we show the results.

1. The e-Science for High Energy Physics

Now science is becoming a team sports. Easy problems are solved and challenging problems require large resources, particularly knowledge from many disciplines [1]. There is an amazing advance in information technology such as Moore's law and widespread use of IT (Information Technology) in science [1]. The e-Science is new R & D paradigm for science which is computationally intensive science that is carried out in highly distributed network environments, or science that uses immense data sets that require grid computing. HEP (High Energy Physics) has a particularly well developed e-Science infrastructure due to their need for adequate computing facilities for the analysis of results and storage of data originating from the CERN LHC (Large Hadron Collider) experiments [2]. HEP is to understand the basic properties of elementary particles and their interactions. HEP is usually conducted at the major accelerator sites, in which detector design, construction, signal processing, data acquisition, and data analysis are performed on a large scale. The size of collaboration is 100~ 2000 physicists. To perform computing at

S.C. Lin and E. Yen (eds.), *Production Grids in Asia: Applications, Developments and Global Ties*, DOI 10.1007/978-1-4419-0046-3_4,
© Springer Science + Business Media, LLC 2010

the required HEP scale, the data grid is a strong requirement [3].

The objective of HEP data grid is to construct a system to manage and process HEP data and to support user group (i.e., high energy physicists). For the current and future HEP activities that require large scale data, the HEP data grid is indispensable and mass storage system of hard disks and tapes in a stable state is necessary. To make the HEP data transparent, CPU power should be extendable and accessible. The transparent HEP data means that the data should be analyzed even if high energy physicists as users do not know the actual place of data [1]. For e-Science for HEP, resources are computers, storage, instrument and network. Middleware resources are LCG (LHC Computing Grid), Linux OS and AIX OS. The applications are ALICE and CDF VO (Virtual Organization). We have been working on e-Science for high-energy physics. We are making ALICE Tier 2 centre and CAF (CDF Analysis Farm) based on LCG farm. In this paper, we introduce the concept of e-Science for high-energy physics and apply the concept to ALICE and CDF experiment. We show the deployment of the concept.

2. The goal of e-Science for High Energy Physics

The goal of e-Science for high-energy physics is to study HEP "anytime and anywhere" even if we are not at accelerator laboratories (on-site). As shown in Figure 1, the components include 1) data production, 2) data processing, and 3) data analysis that can be accessed any time and anywhere even if off-site [3]. First, data production is to get data and take shifts anywhere even if we are not on-site by using a remote operation centre or a remote control room. Second, data processing is to process data by using a HEP data grid. The objective of a HEP data grid is to construct a system to manage and process HEP data and to support the user group (i.e., high energy physicists) [3]. Third, data analysis is for collaborations around world to analyze and publish the results by using collaborative environments.

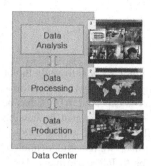

Data Center

Figure 1. The components of e-Science for High Energy Physics.

3. Achievements of e-Science for High Energy Physics

3.1   Data Production

Usually, we take data on-site where accelerators are located. However, in the spirit of e-Science, we would like to take data from anywhere. A method is to use a remote operation centre. An example is the remote operation centre at Fermilab in the USA to operate the LHC experiment at CERN. Currently, we have constructed a remote CDF operation centre at the KISTI, which will enable CDF users in Korea to take CO (Consumer Operator) shifts at the KISTI in Korea, not at Fermilab in USA [3].

Figure 2. Main control room at Fermilab (Left) and the remote control room at the KISTI (Right).

3.2 Data Processing

3.2.1. ALICE data processing

The goal of ALICE experiment at CERN is to study the physics of strongly inter-acting matter at extreme energy densities, where the formation of a new phase of matter, the quark-gluon plasma, is expected. ALICE has been conducted at CERN in which detector design, construction, signal processing, data acquisition, and data analysis are performed. The data size will be a few PBytes data per year. In order to handle this amount of data, we use grid technology. For this work, we as-sembled LCG farm at KISTI for ALICE experiment. The LCG is a world-wide in-frastructure where all the computations relevant to the analysis of the data coming out of the four LHC experiments are taking place. LCG organization involves a hierarchy of computing centres from CERN, labelled Tier1, Tier 2 and Tier 3.

In 2007, the MOST (Ministry of Science and Technology) in Korea and CERN had MOU (Memorandum of Understanding) to build and operate ALICE Tier 2 centre at the KISTI. We have built and operate ALICE Tier2 centre using LCG farms (KR-KISTI-CTRT-01). The ALICE Tier2 centre at the KISTI consists of 120 kSI2K CPU and 30 TBytes of storage. Recently, the farm maintains 96 per-cent operating capacity with 8,000 jobs per month [4]. Now the ALICE Tier2 cen-tre at the KISTI become a federation of global ALICE farms which consists of 13,804 kSI2K CPU and 99.52 PBytes disk around the world [5]. Currently, around 1,000 physicists from 109 institutes, 31 countries use the ALICE farms.

3.2.2 CDF data processing

The CDF is an experiment on the Tevatron in the USA. The CDF detector began its Run II phase in 2001. CDF computing needs are composed of raw data recon-struction and data reduction, event simulation, and user analysis. Although very different in the amount of resources needed, they are all naturally parallel activi-ties. The CDF computing model is based on the concept of CDF Analysis Farm (CAF) [6]. To date, Run II has gathered more than 4 fb^{-1} of data, equivalent to 6.0×10^9 events or a couple of Pbyte of data.

The increasing luminosity of the Tevatron collider causes the computing require-ment for data analysis and MC production to grow larger than the dedicated CPU resources that will be available [7]. In order to meet future demand, CDF is inves-tigating in shared computing resources. The first step is DCAF (Decentralized CDF Analysis Farm) and the final stage is grid. We have first embedded the CAF outside of Fermilab, in Korea called DCAF [8]. Finally we run CDF jobs at LCG farm. Moreover, a significant fraction of these resources is expected to be available to CDF during LHC era and CDF could benefit from using them. In this paper we explain a detailed description of the LCG farm, including both the general idea and the current implementations [9].

The CAF is a large farm of computers running Linux with access to the CDF data handling system and databases to allow the CDF collaborators to run batch analysis jobs [5]. The submission uses a CAF portal which has two special things. The first one is to submit jobs from anywhere. The second thing is that job output can be sent directly to a desktop or stored on CAF FTP server for later retrieval.

However, due to the limited resources of CAF, the CDF experiment produced the concept of the CDF grid. As a first step of grid, we have first suggested and designed the DCAF based on CAF system [10]. A user can submit a job from anywhere to the cluster either at CAF or at the DCAF. DCAF in Korea is much more difficult than CAF due to data files, which are physically apart by more than 10,000 km. In order to run the remote data that is currently stored in Fermilab, USA, we use SAM (Sequential data Access via Meta-data) [11] which consist of Kerberos rcp, bbftp, gridftp and rcp as transfer methods. We use the same GUI (Graphic User Interface) of CAF. The difference is only to select the analysis farm for the DCAF in Korea.

Now, we are in the process of adapting and converting out work flow to the grid. The goal of movement to grid at CDF experiment is world wide trend for HEP experiment. We need to take advantage of global innovations and resources since CDF still has a lot of data to be analyzed.

CAF portal is allowed to change the underlying batch system without changing the user interface. CDF used several batch systems: 1) FBSNG (Fermilab Batch System Next Generation), 2) Condor, 3) Condor over Globus 4) gLite WMS (Workload Management System) [12]. The third and the forth are grid based production system called Grid CAF [12].

The advantage of Condor based grid farm is that all the grid infrastructure is hidden by the glide-ins. The jobs themselves can run both local, dedicated worker nodes and on opportunistic grid resources without any change. Moreover all the advanced features of Condor are preserved [12]. A second advantage comes from the pull model itself. Given that the user job is sent to a worker node only once it is available and tested, the CAF does not have to guess in advance to which queue and on which grid site should it go. In addition, any misconfigured worker node will kill only glide-ins, not user jobs, further raising the success rate [12].

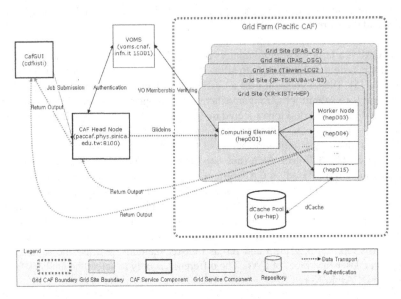

Figure 3. The scheme of Pacific CAF (CDF Analysis Farm).

As shown in Figure 3, we have the federation of LCG/ OSG (Open Science Grid) farm at ASGC in Taiwan, LCG farm at the KISTI in Korea and LCG farm at University of Tsukuba in Japan. We call the federation of grid farm as Pacific CAF.

3.3   Data Analysis

For data analysis collaboration, we host the EVO (enabling virtual organization) server system at the KISTI so that high-energy physicists in Korea may use it directly without using reflectors in USA. Therefore, the EVO server at the KISTI enables collaborations around the world to do analysis and to publish the results together easily [3]. For data analysis collaboration, we have constructed the EVO servers at the KISTI. When users in Korea use the EVO servers at the KISTI, the routing time is reduced by 60 msec without the congestion of the network inside of USA, which gives very stable research environment [3].

4. Achievements with communities

4.1 Achievements with international communities

We have collaborated with many international particle physics and nuclear communities. One of them is FKPPL (France-Korea Particle Physics Laboratory) which has been established on March 2008. The object of FKPPL is to carry out joint cooperative activities, so-called "Joint Research Projects", under a scientific research program in the fields of high-energy physics (notably LHC and ILC) and e-Science including Bioinformatics and related technologies recommended by its Steering Committee.

For the projects of the scientific program are selected from the joint research proposals shown in Table 1.

Table 1. The scientific programs for FKPPL.

Programs	Leading Group	
	France (IN2P3)	Korea (KISTI)
Co-Directors	Vicent Breton, LPC-Clermont Ferrand	Ok-Hwan Byeon, KISTI
Grid Computing	Dominique Boutigny CC-IN2P3	Soonwook Hwang KISTI
ILC Detector R&D	Jean-Claude Brient, LLR-Ecole Polytechnique	Jongman Yang, Ewha Univ.
Bioinformatics	Vincen Breton, LPC-Clermont Ferrand	Doman Kim, Chonnam N. Univ.
ILC Electronics	De La Taille Christophe LAL-IN2P3	Jongseo Chai Sungkyunkwang Univ.
ALICE	Pascal Dupieux, LPC-Clemento Ferrand,	Do-Won Kim, Kangnung N. Univ.

CDF	Aurore Savoy Navarro, LPNHE/ IN2P3-CNRS	Kihyeon Cho, KISTI

We explain an example of CDF project. The goal of this project is to develop the collaboration between the French and Korean computing centres in the area of grid and e-Science. The project has two main dimensions: to integrate KISTI in the LCG and to foster joint research on CDF experiment as one of e-Science applications.

Higher instantaneous luminosity of the Tevatron forced large increases in computing requirements for CDF experiment for both data analysis and MC (Monte Carlo) production needs. Therefore serious efforts were made to be able to access shared, grid, resources over the last two years [13]. LPNHE with CCIN2P3 was involved in the effort to extend the dedicated resource based computing model by using the Condor glide-in mechanism that can create dynamic Condor pools on top of existing batch systems, without any need to install any additional software. All the monitoring tools supported on the dedicated farms, including semi-interactive access to the running jobs and detailed monitoring, have been preserved. Grid CAF was thus born. The first production Grid CAF, developed and deployed at the Tier1 centre at CNAF, Bologna was followed by the deployment of another production GridCAF at the French Tier1 centre at Lyon [13]. The main aim is to collaborate developing this framework at both French Tier1 centre and KISTI.

The other purpose of this project is to collaborate on two fundamental topics in high-energy physics namely the B and Top Physics at the CDF experiment where both teams are participating. B Physics is a major topic where the French IN2P3 team is pursuing its participation especially on the CP violation and Bs mixing. Still important breakthroughs are expected in these coming years. Another topic of interest is to find collaboration on Top Physics. Of special interest is the study of the Top decay into tau lepton which is also instrumental for physics beyond the Standard Model. For these two experimental searches large MC productions will be essential tools [13].

In conclusion, within the framework of this project, KISTI and LPNHE-IN2P3 develop joint research on CDF as one of e-science applications. Research will focus on CDF grid technology and heavy flavour physics [13].

4.2 Achievement with domestic communities

KISTI also provides two CMS (Compact Muon Solenoid) data centres in Korea with international and domestic network. The international network is GLORIAD

(Global Ring Network for Advanced Applications Development) [14] and domestic network is KREONET (Korea Research Environment Open NETwork). One is the CMS Tier2 centre at the KNU (Kyungpook National University). The other is SSCC (Seoul Super Computing Centre) at the University of Seoul.

KNU (Kyungpook National University) has CMS Tier2 Centre. The CMS farm is based on LCG farm. We support 10 Gbps network between CERN to KNU through GLORIAD network and KREONET. The CMS experiment had 'Load Test 2007'. The targets of 'Load Test 2007' are to demonstrate Tier1 centre to each Tier2 centre sustainable at 10 MByte/s for 12 hours and to demonstrate each Tier2 centre to Tier1 centre sustainable at 5 MB/s for 12 hours. KNU has participated in 'Load Test 2007' and met the requirement. KNU has also participated in CSA07 (Computing, Software, and Analysis Challenge). CSA07 showed that the transfer rates of CERN to Tier1 centres are 13 MB/s ~ 105 MB/s depending on Tier1 centres. KNU shows the cumulative transfer volume of 80 TByte during 17 weeks from 36th week of 2007 and 2nd week of 2008 [15].

The University of Seoul has SSCC (Seoul Super Computer Centre) which operates CMS HI (Heavy Ion) data centre. SSCC been established in 2003 with a funding of $1 million [16]. The middleware of SSCC farm is OSG (Open Science Grid) farm since SSCC farm receives CMS HI data from Tier1 centre at Fermilab in USA. Most grid sites in USA is OSG farm since OSG projected is funded by USA government.

5. Conclusions

High-energy physics is one of e-Science top brands at the KISTI. We lead e-Science for high-energy physics in Korea. We succeeded in developing and installing e-Science environment for high-energy physics. For data production, we have run remote control room. For data processing, KISTI is the official ALICE Tier2 centre while KNU is CMS Tier2 centre. KISTI has also participated in CDF experiment and collaborating with Pacific CAF (CDF Analysis Farm) with Taiwan and Japan. For data analysis, we have provided high-energy physics community with EVO sever. Conclusively, high-energy physics plays a major role in e-Science project.

Acknowledgments

We would like to thank to Minho Jeung, Beobkyun Kim and Soonwook Hwang (KISTI) for LCG farm, Yuchul Yang, Mark Neubauer (UCSD) and Frank Wuerthwein (UCSD) for Central Analysis Farm, and Igor Sfillioi (Fermilab) and Hsieh Tsan Lung (ASGC) for Pacific CAF (CDF Analysis Farm).

References

[1]   Kihyeon Cho, Computer Physics Communications 177, 247 (2007).

[2]   The definition of e-Science is from wiki home page
        http://en.wikipedia.org/witk/E-Science..

[3]   Kihyeon Cho, J. of Korean Phys. Soc. 53, 1187 (2008).

[4]   Beobkyun Kim, ALICE Computing, In Proc. of 2008 LHC Physics Workshop at Korea, (Seoul, Korea, 2008).

[5]   See ALICE monitoring system: http://pcalimonitor.cern.ch/reports/.

[6]   M. Neubauer, Nucl. Instr. and Meth. A 502, 386 (2003).

[7]   A.Fella et al, LCGCAF the CDF Protal to the Glite Middleware, In Proc. of Conference on Computing on High Energy Physics (Mumbai, 2006).

[8]   Kihyeon Cho, International Journal of Computer Science and Network Security, Vol.7, No.3, 49 (2007).

[9]   Kihyeon Cho, In proc. of International Symposium on Grid Computing 2007 (Taiwan, 2007).

[10]   K.Cho et al., Construction of DCAF in Korea. In Proc. 18th APAN International Conference Network Research Workshop, (Cairns, 2004); A.Sill et al., Globally Distributed UserAnalysis Computing at CDF. In Proc. of Conference on Computing on High Energy Physics, (Interlaken, 2004).

[11]   G.Garzoglio, SAMGrid project. In Proc. of International HEP Data Grid Workshop, (Daegu, 2002).

[12]   I.Sffligoi, Computer Physics Communications 177, 235 (2007).

[13]   Kihyeon Cho and Aurore Savoy-Navarro, FKPPL Project Application (2008).

[14]   G.Cole, GLORIAD (Global Ring Network for Advanced Applications). In proc. of International ICFA workshop on HEP Networking, Grid and Digital Divide Issues for Global e-Science, (Daegu, 2005).

[15]   Jun-Suhk Suh, CMS Experiment and GLORIAD. In proc. of International Workshop on GLORIAD Networking and Application 2008 (Daejeon, 2008).

[16]   I. Park, CMS-HI Tier2 centre, In Proc. of HPC Asia (Seoul, 2007).

CMS Data Transfer Tests Towards LHC Data taking

Daniele Bonacorsi

University of Bologna, Italy (on behalf of the CMS Collaboration)

Abstract

The CMS experiment has developed a Computing Model designed as a distributed system of computing resources and services relying on Grid technologies. The Data Management part of this model has been established, and it is being constantly exercised and improved through several kind of computing challenged, among which CMS-specific exercises. As LHC starts, CMS will need to manage tens of petabytes of data, thousands of datasets and continuous transfers among 170 CMS Institutions. To get there prepared, in early in 2007 the CMS experiment deployed a traffic load generator infrastructure, aimed at providing CMS Computing Centres (Tiers in the World-wide LHC Computing Grid) with a means for debugging, load-testing and commissioning data transfer routes among them: the LoadTest infrastructure. In addition, a Debugging Data Transfers (DDT) Task Force is being created to coordinate the debugging of data transfer links in the preparation period and during the Computing Software and Analysis challenge in 2007 (CSA07). The task force aims to commission most crucial transfer routes among CMS tiers by designing and enforcing a clear procedure to debug problematic links. Experiences within the CMS LoadTest, standalone and in the context of the first outcomes of the DDT program, are reviewed and discussed.

1. Introduction

The CMS experiment has developed a Computing Model [1, 2] for the computing expected to be needed for the LHC running. In this model, the Data Management components are constantly being exercised and improved through production activities, as well as computing exercises like both WLCG challenges [3] and CMS-wide computing challenges [4]. At the start of LHC, CMS will need to manage tens of petabytes of data, thousands of datasets and continuous transfers among 170 CMS Institutions. The CMS experiment will hence need to sustain uninterrupted high-reliability, high-throughput and very diverse data transfer activities.

S.C. Lin and E. Yen (eds.), *Production Grids in Asia: Applications, Developments and Global Ties*, DOI 10.1007/978-1-4419-0046-3_5,
© Springer Science + Business Media, LLC 2010

2. The CMS Computing Model

The CMS experiment constructed a baseline Computing Model as a distributed system of computing resources and services relying on Grid technologies. The baseline implementation for the Data Management and Workload Management components has been established, along with the main workflows involving the distributed computing facilities, from the Tier-0 centre (T0) and the Analysis Facility at CERN, to 7 Tier-1 centres (T1) and more than 40 Tier-2 centres (T2) located at regional computing sites world-wide. This scheme follows the hierarchical model of computing Tiers as proposed in the MONARC [5] working group and in the first Review of LHC Computing [6, 7].

One of the main technical principles in the design of the CMS Computing Model is to implement a data-driven baseline. Data is partitioned by the experiment as a whole, and do not move around the WAN in response to job submission: all data are placed at big computing centres through explicit CMS policy. This principle leads to a very structured usage of T0 and T1s: they are seen as huge computing resources for the whole experiment, whose activities and functionalities are hence largely predictable since nearly entirely specified. The T0 accepts data from DAQ, performs first-pass prompt reconstruction, provides data archiving capabilities and distributes data to T1s. An Analysis Facility for CMS (currently called CAF) will access full raw dataset and focus on latency-critical activities (detector diagnostics, trigger performance services, derivation of Alignment/Calibration constants). The T1s perform scheduled data-reprocessing and data-intensive tasks (later-pass re-reconstruction, AOD extraction, skimming, etc); data archiving (tape custody of raw+reco and subsequently produced data, as well as Monte Carlo simulated data); disk storage management (fast cache to Mass Storage Systems); data distribution (AOD exchange among T1s, data transfer to T2s for analysis). The T2s are designed as resources for physics analysis, and for Monte Carlo production. While T0 and T1s fulfill the CMS needs for organized mass processing and custodial storage, all the user-driven analysis-oriented unpredictable computing tasks are essentially restricted to the more flexible T2 centres.

3. PhEDEx and CMS data transfers

The CMS data transfer system adopted by CMS is PhEDEx [8, 9]. PhEDEx is responsible for the full range of the CMS transfer needs: from the high-throughput transfers between CERN and the T1 centres, to the high-scale production transfers among T1 and T2 centres, to the management of transfers among all CMS institutions and the provision of straightforward access to handful of files to individual physicists.

The PhEDEx design allows to manage CMS data distribution, for both high-level data subscriptions and managing the interaction with underlying transfer tools. It's design is based on a series of loosely coupled components, which improve the scalability and reliability of data replications. Its distribution infrastructure comprises a set of nodes, operating independently as logical entities given the task of hosting software agents [8]. Such agents are persistent stateless processes, responsible for undertaking specific tasks: they exchange information about system state through a central 'blackboard' (Transfer Management DataBase, TMDB) [8], which contains dataset-replica mappings and locations, dataset subscriptions and allocations, replica set metadata (like size, checksums), transfer states. PhEDEx deploys the blackboard on a high-availability Oracle backend.

The primary concern of PhEDEx is the reliability, regardless of potential fragilities of existing replication tools and services at high loads. PhEDEx provides a scalable infrastructure for managing these operations by automating many low level operations and without imposing constraints on choice of Grid or other distributed technologies. Currently, PhEDEx is fully interfaced with e.g. the File Transfer Service (FTS) as part of the gLite middleware provided by the EGEE project. In order to equip CMS with a system with confirmed capability to meet the objectives, the PhEDEx data transfer system has undergone rigorous development and numerous demanding scale tests [9].

4. Scaling up through computing challenges

The CMS experiment took part in WLCG Service Challenges [3] and in experiment-specific Software, Computing and Analysis (CSA) challenges (an example in [4]), i.e. focussed, sustained testing activities in which most crucial use-cases are exercised. In particular, the data management sector of the CMS Computing Model is being tested: the existing network links and storage systems at Tiers - as well as the Storage Resource Manager (SRM) [10] interfaces - are pushed toward the levels required for running when the LHC experiments come on-line.

After the closure of the WLCG Service Challenge phase 4 (SC4) and after the CMS CSA that ran in 2006 (CSA06), no further WLCG challenges were foreseen in 2007. Nevertheless, CMS intended to continue to constantly put traffic load on the transfer infrastructure, to ramp-up the Tiers towards the demonstration of capability to satisfy the transfer performances needed for LHC data taking.

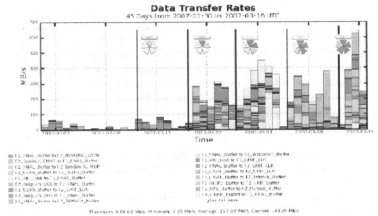

Figure 1 – The LoadTest as a series of "cycles" of testing "weeks".

5. A powerful infrastructure for data transfer testing: the LoadTest design

The CMS experiment deployed early in 2007 a traffic load generator infrastructure, aimed at providing CMS Computing Centres (Tiers in the Worldwide LHC Computing Grid) with a means for debugging, load-testing and commissioning data transfer routes among them. The LoadTest is built upon, and relies on, the PhEDEx system as a reliable data replication tool. On top of PhEDEx, a light file generation and injection procedure was designed and deployed at Tiers to enforce the LoadTest activities.

A CMS computing centre produces its own set of LoadTest fake files, following a set of instructions. A full set corresponds to approximately 700 GB, fragmented into files of 2.6 GB each. Simple and tested procedures - inherited from PhEDEx - are used to inject samples into the PhEDEx database TMDB, and to subscribe destination sites to receive them. The injection rate is adjustable and link dependent, can simulate the T0 output to the T1s and allows to exercise different links with different throughputs. The procedure is such that different sets of logical file names can be injected while actually pointing to the same physical files, hence the availability of test samples at a source site is virtually infinite. To simplify the monitoring and bookkeeping tasks, the LoadTest filenames follow a simple naming convention in which the source site name and the destination site name are part of the name of the injected sample. In addition, in the LoadTest all transfer routes are decoupled: a sample that flows from a site A to a site B (e.g. from a T1 to a T2) is not supposed to flow anywhere else, and can be deleted without affecting any testing activity on other routes. The LoadTest runs using the brand new

PhEDEx priority features, which allow to have both the production data and the test data flowing at the same time in the CMS data transfer topology.

6. Operating the LoadTest infrastructure

To be manageable in daily operations, a simple loop-like operational scheme was introducing. The LoadTest has been organized as several repeated "Cycles" of testing "Weeks" (see Figure 1). In order to guarantee a clean environment, an overall clean-up procedure is usually triggered every Sunday: apart from this scheduled intervention, the LoadTest is configured as a continuously running transfer exercise on a 24/7 basis. Different classes of transfer routes can be identified, and for each a specific testing plan was designed, with the possibility to plug-in site-specific modification as needed or desired by sites. In the LoadTest context, T0-T1 unidirectional transfers, T1-T2 bidirectional "regional" (i.e. with T2's in the same region as the T1) transfers, T1-T2 bidirectional "non regional" transfers and T1-T1 transfers (e.g. also on trans-oceanic network links) were routinely tested, with customizable priorities. The LoadTest was launched in early February 2007 with Cycle-1, and the T0-T1 transfers were soon established (see Figure 2). They smoothly continued through the year, hence the T1 sites were able to exercise their import capabilities, to check the response of SRM interfaces and storage systems to transfers at high loads, and to configure hardware devices and software tools accordingly. The migration to tapes was also exercised, and the HSM at T1s were stress-tested and eventually fine tuned, in preparation to LHC data taking. The involvement of T2s is more delicate, due to their high number, and their different scale of hardware and human resources, as well as know-how, but it was achieved with good results within the first Cycles (see Figure 3).

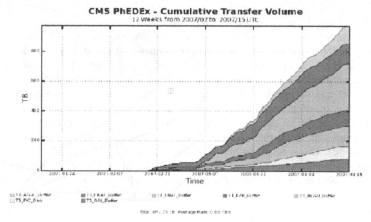

Figure 2 – The T0→T1 tests within the LoadTest activities in 2007.

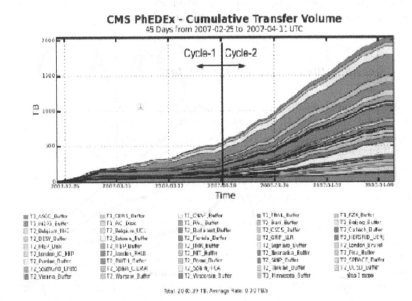

Figure 3 – Evident throughput improvement in T0→T1 testing since the first LoadTest cycles.

All routine activities in the LoadTest were led by the CMS Facilities Infrastructure project, and were managed by a Central Operations Team located at CERN. All site-related operations were performed and followed by CMS contact persons at sites (usually acting as PhEDEx operators as well). The monitoring and visualization features of the PhEDEx system provide an integrated way to overview the LoadTest activities at the same time as production data transfers. The LoadTest Task Force gave feedback to the PhEDEx developers, on real operations scenarios, on ways to collect and analyse common error patterns, to deliver alerts, to take recovery actions, and to assure system consistency and a fast response time to problems. The Central Operations Team shared many responsibilities with the PhEDEx people at the sites. After some weeks of experience, an efficient operations model was designed, in which the central team focused on "global" issues (overall data transfers monitoring and bookkeeping, global troubleshooting, etc) and PhEDEx people at the sites focused on "local" issues (management of PhEDEx instances at Tiers, management of the storage/SRM on-site, local troubleshooting, etc). The synergy within the LoadTest Task Force was achieved via a properly designed communication model, maintained and dynamically adapted by the CMS Facilities and Infrastructure project, which comprises many bilateral communications, use of collaborative web spaces and regular LoadTest weekly meetings.

The LoadTest activities have effectively helped to ramp up the systems and the operations team toward a more mature data operations model, keeping the overall CMS transfer topology under a constant load even if out of a "formal" challenge (see Figure 4). This progress is even more visible in Figure 5, where the total data volume month by month is shown, from early 2004 to Spring 2007.

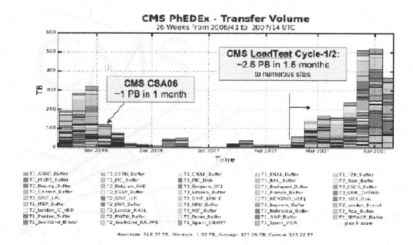

Figure 4 – Overall outcome of the LoadTest activity, compared to CMS CSA06.

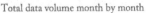

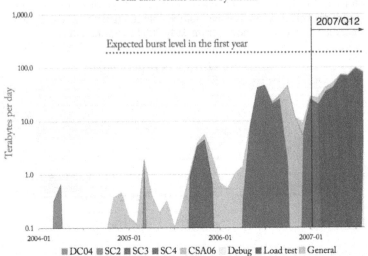

Figure 5 – Ramp-up in the scale of CMS data transfer tests.

7. Status and coming projects

Within the LoadTest activities, PhEDEx demonstrated to be able to sustain production-quality transfers exceeding 1 PB/month for several months and demonstrated core system capacity several orders of magnitude above expected LHC levels. In the first 1.5 months of LoadTest operations, approximately 2.5 PB were moved among CMS Tiers (see Figure 4). The LoadTest infrastructure was proficiently exploited by CMS T1's to address the milestones inherited by the WLCG collaboration (see Figure 6): the system provided a constant data flow to Tiers, and Tiers used it to demonstrate their capability to satisfy the WLCG MoU [11], or at least to quantify their readiness on a clear and useful testing ground. The LoadTest infrastructure was also used by sites to improve their transfer and storage infrastructures and it demonstrated to be a need for improving the systems.

Nevertheless, while Figure 5 shows that CMS approaches the real transfers in scale, Figure 7 shows that CMS is not handling well enough the full complexity, i.e. reliable transfers over the full transfer mesh. While clear improvement in Tiers participation to test transfers since LoadTest started was evident, still not evident improvements in quality could be observed, and a wide span of problems – different in each transfer route – needed to be address to improve this, at a relatively high granularity. For this, the CMS Facilities Infrastructure project, together with the Commissioning projects, launched a Debugging Data Transfer (DDT) program to debug all transfer routes in the PhEDEx topology, thus extending the CMS LoadTest as an important part of the computing preparation activities towards the Computing, Software and Analysis Challenge (CSA07).

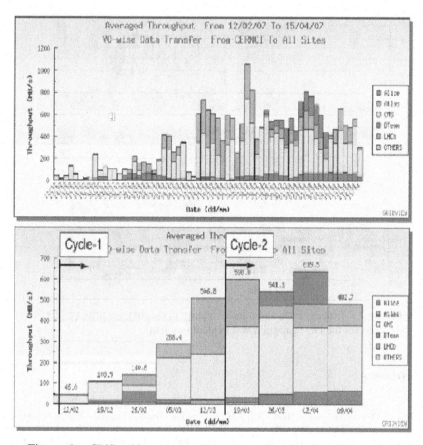

Figure 6 – CMS achievements with the LoadTest infrastructure in the first WLCG multi-VO tests.

In the program, the troubleshooting is done by Tiers, the infrastructural issues are dealt with by the Facilities Operations project, the overall activity is managed by the DDT task force, working on deliverables (e.g. a real-time status map with reasons, of all Tier-to-Tier links; e.g. a number of documented success stories in troubleshooting). Together with the running CCRC08, this effort will provide a unique opportunity to highly improve on CMS transfers in preparation for LHC data taking.

68

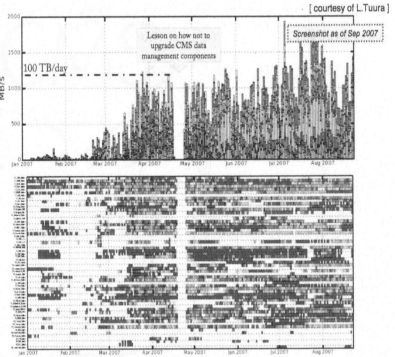

Figure 7 – Transfer rates and transfer quality in the first 3 quarters of 2007: the need for the DDT program was evident (see text).

References

[1]   The CMS Collaboration, "The CMS Computing Model", CERN LHCC 2004-035

[2]   The CMS Collaboration, "The CMS Computing Project - Technical Design Report", CERN-LHCC-2005-023

[3]   D. Bonacorsi, "WLCG Service Challenges and Tiered architecture in the LHC era", IFAE, Pavia, April 2006

[4]   D. Bonacorsi et al, Towards the operation of the INFN Tier-1 for CMS: lessons learned from CMS DC04, in: Proc. ACAT05, DESY Zeuthen, 2005

[5]   M. Aderholz et al., "Models of Networked Analysis at Regional Centres for LHC Experiments (MONARC), Phase 2 Report", CERN/LCB 2000-001

[6]   LHC Computing Grid (LCG) project: http://www.cern.ch/lcg/

[7]   S. Bethke et al., "Report of the Steering Group of the LHC Computing Review", CERN/LHCC 2001-004 (2001)

[8]   T. Barrass et al, Software agents in data and workflow management, in: Proc. CHEP04, Interlaken, 2004. See also http://www.fipa.org

[9]   L. Tuura, B. Bockelman, D. Bonacorsi, R. Egeland, D. Feichtinger, S. Metson, J. Rehn, "Scaling CMS data transfer system for LHC start-up", this conference

[10]   Storage   Resource   Management   (SRM)   project   website, http://sdm.lbl.gov/indexproj.php? ProjectID=SRM

[11]   WLCG Memorandum Of Understanding, CERN-C-RRB-2005-01/Rev, March 2006

CMS Computing Operations at INFN-CNAF with Castor MSS

Daniele Bonacorsi, Andrea Sartirana, Luca Dell'Agnello, Pier Paolo Ricci & Dejan Vitlacil

INFN-CNAF, Bologna, Italy

Abstract

The CMS experiment is preparing for the real LHC data handling by building and testing its Computing Model in periodic challenges of increasing scale and complexity. INFN-CNAF is one of 7 national level Tier-1 centres playing a key role in the management and distribution of the CMS experiment data. During the last years, leveraging on the feedback of various computing challenges, a great effort was spent in defining and commissioning INFN-CNAF services and operations in order to support CMS activities. In particular, the data management operations on a Castor MSS system where widely tested. This note describes the setup of Castor MSS at CNAF. In particular, the results of the tests performed during the phase-1 of CCRC'08 (Common-VO Computing Readiness Challenge 2008) are reported and discussed.

3. *Introduction*

The CMS experiment is preparing for the LHC data taking by testing its Computing Model [1, 2] in daily production-quality operations at the regional level as well as in scheduled CMS-wide challenges of considerable complexity [3].

In the CMS Computing Model, a Tier-1 centre has a crucial role. It accepts and store RAW+RECO data from the Tier-0 and grants data archiving capabilities (tape custody of RAW+RECO and subsequently produced data in the region); it performs scheduled data reprocessing and data-intensive tasks (later-pass re-reconstruction, AOD extraction, skimming, etc), as well as disk storage management (fast cache to Mass Storage Systems) and inbound/outbound data distribution (AOD exchange among Tier-1 centres, data transfer to Tier-2 centres for analysis, and from Tier-2 centre to store the outcome of Monte Carlo productions). All computing challenges and tests over last few years have brought to a more and more deep insight on most crucial issues for successful Tier-1 operation with real data within the overall CMS computing infrastructure. In particular, for the first

S.C. Lin and E. Yen (eds.), *Production Grids in Asia: Applications, Developments and Global Ties*, DOI 10.1007/978-1-4419-0046-3_6,
© Springer Science + Business Media, LLC 2010

time on February 2008, the CCRC'08 (Common-VO Computing Readiness Challenge 2008) exercise performed a throughout test of the contemporaneous activity of all the 4 LHC experiments. This brought a priceless feedback on the operational setup at the Tier-1 centres, in particular at those multi-VO centres that are supporting the activity of more than one LHC experiment.

The Italian Tier-1 centre is located at the INFN-CNAF Computing Centre. The data management operations on a Castor MSS system were widely stressed and tested on-site during the last challenges, as well as during the ramping up of daily operations in sight of the data taking. In the following we will give a brief description of the Castor MSS system deployed at CNAF as well as describe and discuss the tests on the storage system which were performed during the Phase-I of CCRC challenge.

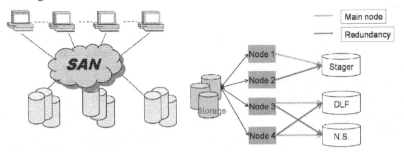

Figure 1 – Pictorial, qualitative view of CNAF Storage Area Network and Castor nodes configuration

3. *Castor set-up at INFN-CNAF Tier-1*

The main resource for data storage at CNAF consists of a Castor Hierarchical Storage Manager (HSM) system [4], at version 2.1.6 at the time of this Symposium. The Castor system is developed at CERN and is primarily used to store physics production files and user files over different Tiered layers of mass storage. It consists of at least 2 different layers, the disk storage - which is used as a data buffer with fast access - and the tape backend, with greater capacity but higher latency. The Castor deployment set-up is fully covered in [5], and is briefly outlines in the following.

The tape backend resides on a Storagetek silos L5500 Robot tape Library managed by a dedicated software running over a dedicated Sun Blade v100 with 2 internal IDE disks with software RAID1. The Sun Blade runs the ACSLS 7.0 with OS Solaris 9.0, which is the dedicated software that manages the tape drive mount and dismount operations besides the tape library robot monitoring and general support activity. The tape library is partitioned in 2 form-factor slots, corresponding to about 2000 slots LTO-2 form and about 3500 slots 9940B form respectively, equipped with 200 GB cartridges, for a total capacity of 1.1 PB of uncompressed tape capacity. In general, High Energy Physics users do store on the Castor system data that are already compressed or with a very low compressibility ratio, so the 1.1 PB capacity should be intended as real available space.

Each tape drive is accessed using the LAN with a dedicated server machine (the so called "tape-server"); this machine is connected with a dedicated Ethernet 1Gb/s connection to the Local Network, and with a specific Fiber Channel (FC) HBA to the tape drive. In total, 16 tape drives (mixed LTO-2 and 9940B) with 2 Gb/s Fiber Channel interface, are installed and shared among the supported Virtual Organizations. A number of ~10 tape-servers, namely 1U Supermicro 3 GHz with 4GB of RAM, 1Qlogic 2300 FC HBA, Storagetek CSC Development Toolkit provided by CERN (the Toolkit needed to act as client for the ACSLS software with a license agreement with Storagetek) are installed and directly connected with the FC drive output. The disk data are accessed in a similar way with dedicated machines (the so called "disk-servers") acting as front-ends to the disk storage on Storage Area Network.

A set of ~40 disk-servers with hardware 1U Supermicro 3 GHz with 4GB of RAM, 1 Qlogic 2300 FC HBA accessing the CNAF SAN (see Figure 1) and running *rfiod* are installed. Among these, 15 disk-servers are dedicated to the unique CMS T1D0 class, for a total disk space of 124 TB. The garbage collector threshold, which is the limit under which the older data on the disk buffer are deleted, is at 10-15%. The storage hardware boxes are STK FlexLine 600, IBM FastT900, EMC Clarion; all these storage boxes consists of dual redundant RAID controllers with at least double data paths to the SAN and the mass storage resides on ATA disk expansions of different capacity (principally 250GB and 500GB) connected to the controllers.

The Castor central machine is a IBM x345 2U machine 2x3GHz Intel Xeon, raid1 with double power supply, with Red Hat A.S. 3.0. It runs all central Castor services (*nsdaemon, vmgrdaemon, cupvdaemon, vdqmdaemon, msgdaemon*) and the Oracle client for the central database (see Figure 1). A Dell 1650 R.H 7.2 runs Castor monitoring service (Cmon daemon) and Nagios central service for monitoring and notification, plus interface commands to the tape-servers. A 1U Supermicro 3 GHz with 4GB of RAM, 1 Qlogic 2300 FC HBA accessing the CNAF SAN and running the Castor-2 stager, namely *cdbdaemon, stgdaemon* and *rfiod* is available.
High availability, scalability, reliability is achieved through a modular architecture based on the following building blocks: Oracle Real Application Cluster (RAC): the database is shared across several nodes with failover and load balancing capabilities; Oracle ASM for storage management: implementation of redundancy and striping in an Oracle oriented way. Castor uses 4 Oracle databases (DLF, Stager, Nameserver, repack), with 5 servers, 64bit 2*Xeon dual core, 8GB ram, 300 GB disks, all accessing the same physical storage. The total is 1.2 TB (2.4 TB RAW) for databases and 1.2 TB (2.4 TB RAW) for backup. The stager exploits a RAC

system with 2 nodes (servers), no load balancing, 2nd server only for failover (according to CERN suggestions, see Figure 1). The Name Server exploits a RAC system with 2 nodes (shared with DLF), 2nd node only failover. The DLF exploits a RAC system with 2 nodes (shared with NameServer), 1st node only failover.

The SRM [6] set-up consists of a dedicated SRMv2 endpoint (*srm-v2-cms.cr.cnaf.infn.it*) with 3 servers (2 FE + 1 BE) and a dedicated SRMv1 endpoint (*castorsrm.cr.cnaf.infn.it*), with 3 servers - now being phased-out.

3. Use of Castor in CMS transfer tests in CCRC/phase-1

During the phase 1 of the WLCG Common-VO Computing Readiness Challenge in 2008 (CCRC'08), a complete set of transfer test was performed involving the Castor storage and the newly deployed SRMv2 endpoint. The tests relied on the CMS LoadTest infrastructure, based on the PhEDEx [7] data transfer system in use by CMS. The CCRC/phase-1 metrics for test transfers in CCRC/phase-1 in the INFN region were:

- T0-CNAF transfers: at 40% of 2008 target (29MB/s), 50% optimal (37MB/s), 25% threshold (18MB/s), for 3 days in a row;
- CNAF-T1 transfers: at 50% of 2008 target to at least 3 T1s, among which one in another continent;
- CNAF-T2 transfers: to regional T2s only (4 INFN T2 + Wien T2 + Budapest T2) at defined target rates for at least 3 days in a row (34,2 MB/s [INFN], 10,3 MB/s [Budapest], 8,4 MB/s [Wien]).

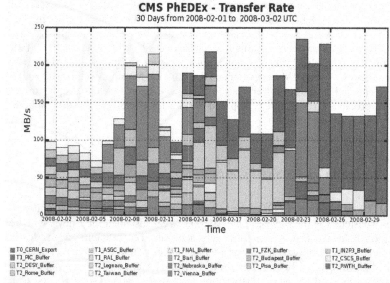

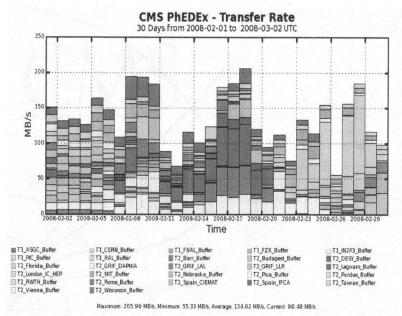

Figure 2 – CMS results achieved in CCRC'08/phase-1 in terms of overall inbound (top) and outbound (bottom) WAN traffic.

The main problems encountered were SRMv2 overload problems. An excess of disk-server slots kept busy caused the incoming SRM calls to stay queues in Castor-LSF; the FTS timeouts on Prepare-to-Get and/or Prepare-to-Put calls are tipically 300 sec; as a consequence this problem may easily lead to nearly 100% failures. The LoadTest load was eased and, after some intervention of CNAF storage experts together with SRMv2 developers, the situation has improved considerably. At the end, all CCRC transfer tests metric have been reached despite initial SRMv2 problems (see Figure 2, top and bottom for overall CNAF inbound and outbound traffic respectively).

3.   Migration and Stage-in tests

During T0->T1 tests in CCRC/phase-1, also the *tape migration* of the imported data was tested. The metrics was 25% of 2008 target sustained for 3 days, with no migration holes >6 hrs. All metrics were achieved, but problems were clearly identified. The migration spread over a large number of tapes, which prevented an efficient clean-up after the test. The need of more efficient tape writing policy was identified. The need of constant babysitting from storage administrators persists in Castor. In particular, migration can be constant only by restarting Migration Streams every few hrs and this would not be acceptable in a true data-taking period. This issue has been actually addressed with the following version of CASTOR (v. 2.1.7).

The goal of the *stage-in tests* was to measure latency, throughput and success rate for Tape to Buffer stage-in, for files that are only kept on Tape (not on disk). Results might be site-dependent and would give an idea of reconstruction success in case of no pre-staging at sites. The test was designed so to select one (or more) dataset(s) of ~10 TB size existing at T1's, to remove all the files from disk buffer, to fire the staging from Tape to Buffer of all files, to monitor and measure the process. The results for CNAF are shown in Table 1 and Figure 3.

Data volume [TB]	# files	# tapes	<# files> /tape	stage-in request time [min]	Total stage-in time [hrs]	Tape to buffer [MB/s]	<files> per mount	Total # mounts	File failures [%]
10.8	7235	426	17	~45	79	~40	2.1	3406	7.6

Table 1 – CNAF measurement from the first global stage-in test ever done on-site by one experiment, by CMS during phase 1 of CCRC'08.

The data was found to be spread over a high number of tapes despite the choice was for datasets migrated to tape in the same period. In addition, many tapes had very few files (<files/tape> =~17). Nevertheless, the test was done in 44 hours (67.0 MB/s in Tape to Buffer transfers). Although, there were about 2 days in which 57 problematic files were the only one left and they were recalled over and over. As a consequence, averaging on the total time of the test (79 hours), the peak rate above turns into the average rate of 37.5 MB/s. Moreover, it was observed that some disk-servers went in "stack overflow" during the test (caused by the overall CMS activity); additionally, one storage device was lost for hardware failure, and the corresponding data had to be re-staged on other disk-servers.

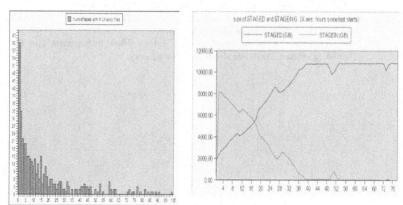

Figure 3 – CNAF results achieved in stage-in tests during CCRC'08/phase-1. On the left, file occupancy on tapes. On the right, size of the staged-in (blue and being staged-in (pink) files versus time (in hours).

It is interesting to mention that CNAF ran this exercise in parallel with other activities: e.g. CMS had a heavy read/write activity due to transfer and processing; in addition, ATLAS was migrating data to tapes at the same time. This means that during the exercise the recall test was actually sharing tape-servers with other activities, and conflicting with other activities for disk-servers free slots: so it was indeed a real-life test for a multi-VO T1. On the other hand, it was not designed to achieve the maximum performance, but to measure bottlenecks: e.g., the low number of staged-in files per mount reveals an evident inefficiency in stage-in, and hence the need for a a-priori more organized data writing to tapes, i.e. the need for implementing tape families on Castor storage at CNAF.

Moreover CNAF MSS is going to be upgraded with a second, more scalable library, an SL8500 supporting 1 TB tapes (hence leading to a minor spreading of data across tapes) and more performing drives.

References

[1]   The CMS Collaboration, "The CMS Computing Model", CERN LHCC 2004-035

78

[2]   The CMS Collaboration, "The CMS Computing Project - Technical Design Report",
        CERN-LHCC-2005-023

[3]   D. Bonacorsi et al, "WLCG Service Challenges and Tiered architecture in the LHC
        era", IFAE, Pavia, April 2006

[4]   Castor software: http://castor.web.cern.ch/castor/

[5]   G. Lo Re et al, "Storage resources management and access at CNAF Tier-1",
        ACAT'05 Conference, Nucl. Instrum. Meth. NIM-A 559 (2006) 62-66

[6]   Storage   Resource   Management   (SRM)   project   website,
        http://sdm.lbl.gov/indexproj.php?ProjectID=SRM

[7]   T. Barrass et al, "Software agents in data and workflow management", in Proc.
        CHEP04, Interlaken, 2004. See also http://www.fipa.org

Distributed Computing and Data Analysis for CMS in View of the LHC Startup

Peter Kreuzer

RWTH-Aachen IIIa, Switzerland

Abstract

The Large Hadron Collider (LHC) at CERN/Geneva is about to deliver first collision data to the CMS experiment. The CMS computing, software and analysis projects will need to meet the expected performances in terms of archiving of raw detector data, prompt calibration and primary reconstruction at the host laboratory, data distribution and handling at Tier-1 centres, data access and distributed physics analysis at Tier-2 centres. Hundreds of physicists located in nearly 200 institutions around the world will then expect to find the necessary infrastructure to easily access and process experimental data, including a large range of activities from low-level detector performance evaluation to involved discovery physics analysis. In the past two years, CMS has conducted computing, software, and analysis challenges to demonstrate the functionality, scalability, and usability of the computing and software components. These challenges have been designed to validate the CMS distributed computing model by demonstrating the functionality of many components simultaneously. We will present the major boost demonstrated by CMS in event processing, data transfers and analysis processing during the CSA07 and ongoing CCRC08 data challenges. In particular, we will describe relevant functional tests and the scale achieved from each CMS component and externally provided component. We will also summarize the main physics analysis lessons drawn from these challenges and the on-going tunings for an optimal begin of the experiment. We inform the reader that the present report contains updated results from the year 2008 in comparison with those presented during the conference.

5. Introduction

Soon after first LHC collisions will occur, more than 2300 CMS collaborators located in 40 countries around the world will expect to be able to carry out their final physics analysis with minimal geographical and processing constraints, ideally on their portable computer. Such a a non-trivial expectation on data processing and data distribution has been addressed in recent years via the design, develop-

S.C. Lin and E. Yen (eds.), *Production Grids in Asia: Applications, Developments and Global Ties*, DOI 10.1007/978-1-4419-0046-3_7,
© Springer Science + Business Media, LLC 2010

ment and deployment of the tiered computing model, on top of the World Wide LHC Grid (WLCG) infrastructure. The CMS Computing model as depicted in Fig. 1 is designed to handle O(1-10PB) data per year, to be delivered in most transparent manner to the physics community located around the world. The primary data archival and the prompt reconstruction are done at the Tier-0; time-critical calibration and alignment, and high-priority analysis work-flows are done at the CERN Analysis Facility (CAF). A second custodial copy of the primary data is split and sent to Tier-1s for storage; the latter sites also re-process the data once improved detector conditions data are available and perform a secondary event selection of interesting physics channels, to be sent to Tier-2s for analysis. In parallel to physics analysis, Tier-2s are also responsible for the production of simulation data, which in turn is sent back for storage to their "regional" Tier-1.

The CMS Computing infrastructure has grown significantly in recent years, comprising in Fall 2008 a number of 7 Tier-1s and ☐40 Tier-2s, for a total of ☐20,000 cores computers, ~15 PB disk and ~15 PB tape capacity. The unexpected delay in the LHC startup due to a machine incident did not stop the CMS Computing and Physics communities from testing their models during 2008 via so called "data challenges" and by processing over 600 Millions cosmic muon events. In Sect. 2 we summarize the most significant metrics achieved at all levels of the distributed computing infrastructure; we also describe the operational progress made while processing cosmic runs in sustained data taking mode. In Sect. 3 and 4 we describe in details the CMS user analysis tools and performance.

5. Achieved metrics in CMS distributed computing

In the last 4 years, CMS has carried out a series of Computing, Software & Analysis (CSA) data challenges, with the goal to (1) operate the system in quasi-real data taking conditions and (2) scale the distributed computing resources up to the design level. The goals of the CSA08 data challenge was to simulate the first 3 months of CMS data taking, including the demonstration of key use case performances of the Tier-0, the CAF, the Tier-1 and the Tier-2 infrastructure. In parallel, the WLCG project carried out a Combined Computing Readiness Challenge (CCRC08), stressing-testing portions of the grid infrastructure used simultaneously by all 4 LHC experiments, e.g. parallel data transfers out of CERN or parallel processing at multi-VO sites[1.]

---

[1] A "multi-VO" site is serving multiple virtual organizations, e.g. multiple LHC experiments or other scientific communities.

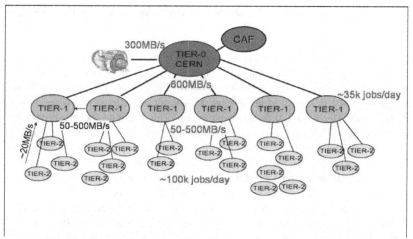

Fig. 1- The CMS tiered Computing Model: work-flows at various Tier levels are described in the text. The throughput figure out of Tier-0 represent the aggregate design value, while the other throughput figures are design ranges, depending on the sites resources.

2.1   CMS Tier-0 and CAF processing performance

The CMS Tier-0 is responsible for handling the data in the first period of its life: after being written by the CMS data acquisition system to a disk buffer near the experimental area[2] [2], the data is transferred in form of binary streams to a CASTOR disk pool at CERN via a single 10Gbit link, where it is repacked into primary physics datasets and merged into complete luminosity sections; the data is then stored on tape and exported to one of the Tier-1 centres. After 24h at maximum, the first reconstruction pass over all data starts, which are in turned archived and sent to Tier-1s. The CMS Tier-0 is designed to handle data from the detector at a steady rate of 300MB per second, with bursts of 1GB per second. During the 2008 cosmic data taking, CMS has successfully maintained repacking at twice the design rate (600MB per second) and during the CSA08 data challenge, the Tier-0 batch farm has demonstrated a sustained number of processing jobs close to the saturation level of 2,200 job-slots, see Fig. 2. The main limitations encountered during 2008 Tier-0 processing were related to too long jobs (up to 24h) and too large output data files, since the current design requires a complete luminosity section per datafile. There are plans to process the reconstruction step in parallel and then have a datafile merging at the end, hence reducing the overall latency. The

---

[2] the CMS experiment is located opposite to CERN along the 27 kilometer circumference LHC circle

large file size issue can be addressed by a sensible definition of primary physics datasets.

The CAF was designed to host a large variety of latency-critical work-flows at CERN, in particular calibration and alignment processes based on dedicated streams sent by Tier-0 with a fast-turnaround of ☐1 hour. The output of these processes results in improved knowledge of detector conditions, which are in turn fed back into Tier-0 for full data reconstruction. This chain has been successfully tested during the CSA08 data challenge, for example for the tracker alignment procedure as shown in Fig. 3. The CAF further hosts detector commissioning and diagnosis work-flows, in particular based on raw datasets, as well as high-interest physics analysis requiring fast-turnaround. The resource requirements include a large batch farm (650 cores) and a large CASTOR disk pool (1.2 PB) with efficient data access patterns. These resources have been deployed and successfully commissioned during 2008. Nearly 250 users have been active on the CAF, requiring a solid resource management and user support. No major limitation has been encountered, although the CAF activity is partially unpredictable, since heavily dependent on commissioning and analysis needs which can rapidly evolve. This can be addressed by further strengthening the CPU, Disk and user management.

2.2 CMS Data Transfer performance

A mandatory requirement on any worldwide distributed Computing model is a reliable data transfer system and infrastructure. The well established CMS transfer tool PhEDEx [2], [4] is based on a set of agents running in all CMS sites and laying on top of central ORACLE data base; the tool allows any CMS collaborator to request a data transfer to any CMS site, which only needs to be approved by the corresponding site data manager. Each transfer link from CERN to Tier-1s consist of a dedicated 10Gbit optical network, while other links are using general purpose networking. Since most Tier-1 sites are serving several LHC experiments simultaneously, testing the aggregated transfer band-with from CERN to Tier-1s represented a crucial goal of the CCRC08 challenge.

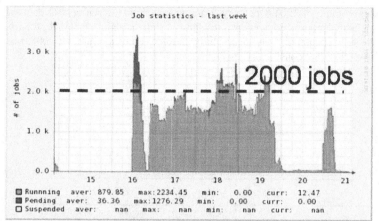

Fig. 2 - CMS Prompt reconstruction jobs running on the Tier-0 during the Computing, Software & Analysis (CSA08) data challenge.

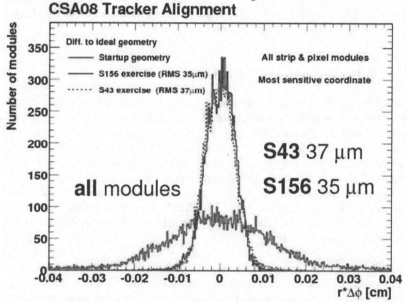

Fig. 3- CMS Tracker Alignment procedure on the CERN Analysis Facility during the Computing, Software & Analysis (CSA08) data challenge. The resolution is shown before and after the alignment procedure.

As shown in Fig. 4, CMS routinely reached its nominal aggregated band-with of 600MB per second. CMS is also commissioning the full mesh of Tier-ik-Tier-jl links, hence minimising the geographical constraints on the data accessibility. An efficient collaboration between central CMS operations and CMS sites started in 2007 and resulted in a few hundreds of commissioned links and an average trans-

84

fer data volume of 120TB per day. Data consistency between central data bases and the actual storage contents at sites showed to be a major challenge, for which a dedicated "campaign" was successfully carried out during Summer 2008, resulting in reliable data consistency checking tools.

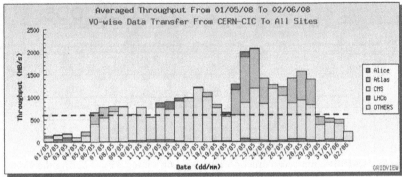

Fig. 4 - Data throughput out of CERN during the WLCG Combined Computing Readiness Challenge (CCRC08). The aggregate CMS band-with to all Tier-1 routinely reached the nominal 600MB per second.

2.3 CMS Tier-1 re-processing performance

The CMS Tier-1 computing centres are located at large universities and national laboratories; they host a second custodial copy of the raw data and the primary copy of the simulated data; they need data serving capacity to Tier-2 centres for analysis and host the bulk of re-processing and event selection for the experiment. The Tier-1 sites have a challenging role in CMS because they are expected to ingest and archive data from both CERN and regional Tier-2 centres, while they export data to a global mesh of Tier-2s at rates comparable to the raw export data rate from CERN. The combined capacity of the Tier-1 centres is more than twice the resources located at CERN and efficiently utilizing this large distributed resources is a challenge.

In 2008, valuable experience was gained in operating and utilizing the CMS Tier-1 computing centres, in particular through the stable operations of CMS services, the ability to scale to large numbers of processing requests and large volumes of data, and the ability to provide custodial storage and high performance data serving.

The standard CMS data processing tool "ProdAgent" running at Tier-1s consists of a set of Python-based modules on top of MySQL data bases; each module contains a functional piece of the system, e.g. merging small data files, running the CMS simulation or reconstruction framework or injecting output data into the transfer system. A main challenge of the Tier-1 work-flow is file-based processing, hence heavily relying on the local storage and staging infrastructure. No major bottle neck was found. Another interesting feature is the ability to access both raw and reconstructed data information in the same "skimming" job, in order to efficiently select interesting physics channels and reduce the amount of data for further analysis of the data at Tier-2s. Skimming work-flows have been successfully tested. During the CSA08 data challenge, the seven CMS Tier-1 routinely ran re-processing and skimming work-flows, by actively using the jobs-slots available to CMS. No major limitation was observed regarding the CPU fair-share settings in multi-VO Tier-1 centres, however a more sustained processing period is needed to confirm this observation.

2.4 Central Computing Operations experience

The other essential aspects of distributed computing in view of the LHC startup are related to central computing operations and their collaboration with all CMS sites. Besides the traditional control room near the experimental area, CMS has deployed 2 major offline computing control rooms - the CMS Centre at CERN and the CMS Remote Operation Centre at the Fermi National Physics Laboratory in Chicago/USA - from where all distributed work-flows are controlled and monitored: both the Tier-0 and the CAF have caughtmost operational attention in the early cosmic data taking phase, as well as the distributed Tier-1 centres, which have been routinely operated centrally from a distance for transferring data, submitting data serving requests, and submitting batch processing requests. Site Availability Monitoring (SAM) tools, computing shift procedures and central ticketing services have been strengthened throughout the 2008 data challenges and cosmic data taking periods. Improvements can still be made in terms of communication between central computing and sites, as well as further automation in the monitoring and alarming systems, in order to reduce the load on individual operators when sustained LHC data taking will start. A stronger focus also needs to be given to Tier-2 infrastructure and data transfer monitoring.

3. Data driven analysis model

CMS Data analysis is performed in a distributed environment, using the grid infrastructure. A very large amount of data needs to be distributed to many Tier2 centres located in many different countries; the data distribution to a Tier-2 is done according to its pre-defined association to Physics Analysis Groups and to the resources reserved to a local Tier-2 community.

This model foresees that jobs are submitted to remote analysis resources where data are hosted, transparently to the CMS end-user who needs minimal knowledge of the underlying infrastructure.

3.1 Data analysis work-flow

The CMS analysis model has been organized in three main steps. The user runs interactively over small data samples in order to develop and test her/his code, using the CMS analysis framework (CMSSW). Once ready, the user typically needs higher statistics, hence access to part of or the whole dataset, which has been already distributed to Tier2 resources. The produced output data are moved to Tier-2s according to central Physics Analysis Group space, regional or local user space. At the end the produced output must be made available to the user, in order to perform final analysis and plots. A schema of the described flow is shown in Fig. 5. The related work-flow can be factorized as follows:

•Data Discovery step: Interacting with the CMS data management infrastructure, to find out about the existence and the location of the input data;

•Interaction with the CMSSW analysis framework: testing on local machine, so that the very same environment can be reproduced once the analysis is sent to remote resources;

•Grid specific step: Performing all actions from submission to output retrieval.

For the latter step CMS has developed the CMS Remote Analysis Builder (CRAB) [3], in order to provide transparency to the structure of the computing system.

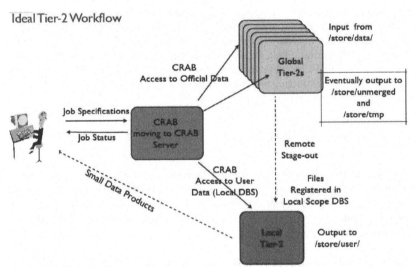

Fig. 5 - CMS Analysis work-flow schema, showing the related interaction points between theWorkload Management and the Data Management tools.

3.2 Data Discovery

One of the crucial aspect of the distributed analysis is to allow physicists to discover available event data. The CMS catalogs used to define and discover data are the Dataset Bookkeeping System (DBS) and the Data Location Service (DLS). DBS maintains the semantic information associated to datasets, keeps track of the data parentage and allows to discover which data exist and how they are organized in terms of files/file-blocks. DLS maps file-blocks to sites hosting a replica and finds the location of desired data. DBS supports the existence of local and global instances, for "private" and "public" data, and the migration of data between them.

DBS and DLS are integrated in a single service that is implemented as a Tomcat-based Java server with an Oracle or MySQL back-end. CMS also uses a local file catalog which provides access information for the files at the site storage, with simple rules to build physical paths from logical names and access protocols. CMS applications interact with the local storage via a POSIX-like interface [4].

3.3 CMS Remote Analysis Builder

CRAB has been designed for CMS physicists to efficiently access distributed data and hide the underlying complexity of grid infrastructure. Following the above described analysis model, a User Interface is provided to CRAB users, containing grid client middle-ware in order to access word wide distributed data. Once a specific user analysis code has been developed and tested the user only needs to interact with CRAB configuration parameters, e.g. the input dataset name, the specific analysis configuration, etc. The rest of the work-flow is handled by CRAB, namely: interaction with the CMS Data Management infrastructure, interactions with the CMSSW Framework on local machine, in order to reproduce the same environment on the remote resources and obviously all the grid specific steps. These are implemented in CRAB via a client-server architecture, where the server, placed between the user and the grid, has the role to perform all the actions, from submission to output retrieval.

The main goals of the client-server architecture is to automate as much as possible the whole analysis work-flow and to improve the scalability and reliability of the system.

5. *Distributed Analysis activity in CMS*

The CMS collaboration has been performing data analysis through the grid infra-structure with success for more than three years. The first intensive usage of the analysis tool by a large number of users at different locationswas achieved during Spring 2006 analysis round as input to the CMS Physics Technical Design Report [5].

Within such a complex infrastructure, scaling tests are one of the most crucial factor for deploying the whole system: such tests have been carried out during the various CMS data challenges. During the CCRC08 challenge, a dedicated analysis test was organized, based on simulated events.More than 100,000 jobs on □30 Tier-2 sites were submitted during two weeks through the CRAB server. More-over, the distributed analysis model was successfully used by a large amount of CMS collaborators during the cosmic data taking, in particular by accessing real data made available at many sites.

4.1 Users activity

In 2008, the size of the CMS physics community daily interacting with the analy-sis infrastructure has been constantly increasing: since January 2008 there were about 800 distinct users who submitted □9Millions analysis jobs. In Fig. 6 the cumulative number of distinct CMS users which submitted analysis jobs through the distributed infrastructure via CRAB is shown. The user activity is also an im-portant measure for testing the actual CRAB server scalability and reliability: so far no limitation has been identified while serving about 50 users and an average of 30,000 jobs per day with a single CRAB server. A more consistent and precise error reporting between the software framework and CRAB can further improve the user-support activity.

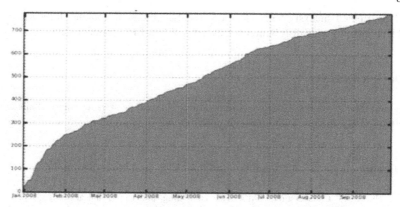

Fig. 6 Cumulative plots of distinct CMS users submitting analysis jobs through the grid infrastructure in 2008.

As mentioned above, the CMS analysis tools are designed to make the complex distributed infrastructure nearly transparent to the end-user. Let's take the example of a CMS physics simulation in the SUSY sector, with O(1 TB) selected ("skimmed") signal and background events. Independently of her/his geographical location, the end-user has to be able to access these data many times at the Tier-2 centres where they are stored, e.g. Tier-2s associated to the CMS SUSY Physics Analysis Group. The output histograms of each analysis round are sent back to the end-user's computer via the CRAB machinery, with an overall turnaround of typically 1 day for O (1 TB) input data, including data analysis and transfer. The increasing amount of CMS physicists using the distributed analysis infrastructure proves the success of the model and confirms that a solid user support service is required, in order to scale to with the expected analysis traffic once LHC collision data will be available.

5. Conclusions

The CMS Computing infrastructure and operation have been substantially upscaled and tested in recent years. The most crucial design metrics have been demonstrated during data challenges and cosmic data taking in 2008, including first pass reconstruction of the data at he host laboratory (CERN), data transfer throughput, distributed Tier-1 processing and Tier-2 analysis work-flows, routinely achieving a total of 100,000 jobs per day, see Fig. 7. In view of the LHC startup, additional challenges and goals will be a potentially larger requirement on Tier-0 input data rates (up to 2GB per second); a sustained and simultaneous processing of all distributed computing work-flows, requiring improved automation in monitoring and alarms; finally the number of user analysis activities is expected to further ramp up with the LHC startup, hence further challenging the data serving

90

and distributed analysis tools. The CMS collaboration is looking forward to achieving world-wide distribution and analysis of first LHC collision data.

Acknowledgements

I would like to thank Georgia Karapostoli (Univ.Athens/Greece) and Daniele Spiga (INFN Perugia/CERN) for their contributions to this report.

References

[1]. The CMS Collaboration: CMS: The computing project. Technical design report, CERNLHCC- 2005-023, Jun 2005. 166pp.

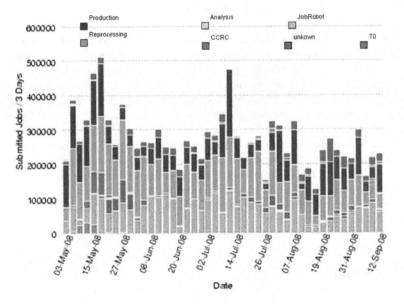

Fig. 7 - Overall CMS jobs running at various level of the distributed grid infrastructure. The vertical scale refers to a 3-days binning.

[2]. T. Barrass et al : Software Agents in Data and Workload Management, Published in *Interlaken 2004, Computing in high energy physics and nuclear physics* 838-841 Proceedings of the CHEP04 Conference. Interlaken, Switzerland, September 27th.

[3]. D.Spiga et al. : The CMS Remote Analysis Builder (CRAB), Lecture notes in computer science, 2007. vol. 4873, pp. 580-586

[4]. A. Delgado Peris et al. : Data location, transfer and bookkeeping in CMS, 18th Hadron Collider Physics Symposium 2007 (HCP 2007) 20-26 May 2007, La Biodola, Isola d'Elba, Italy. Published in Nucl.Phys.Proc.Suppl.177-178:279-280, 2008.

[5]. CMS Collaboration : CMS Physics TDR, Volume II, J. Phys. G: Nucl. Part. Phys. 34 995-1579

Grid Technologies for Cancer Research in the ACGT Project

Juliusz Pukacki[1] & Dennis Wegener [2]

[1] Poznan Supercomputing and Networking Centre, Poland
[2] Fraunhofer IAIS, Germany

Abstract

The ACGT project focuses on the domain of cancer research with the ultimate objective to design, development and validation of an integrated grid-enabled platform supporting post-genomic, multi-centric clinical trials on cancer.
The purpose of this paper is to describe the role of grid technologies in the ACGT environment. The paper gives details on the grid-related parts of the ACGT system architecture and its advantages, e.g. a unified authorization framework.
In addition, two examples on how the grid environment is used within ACGT are presented: the oncosimulator, which is a standalone application that requires a lot of computational power to simulate tumor growth, and the GridR toolkit, which is a grid-enabled version of well known R environment

1   Introduction

ACGT focuses on the domain of cancer research with the ultimate objective to design, development and validation of an integrated grid-enabled platform supporting post-genomic, multi-centric clinical trials on cancer. The driving motivation behind the project is our committed belief that the breadth and depth of knowledge already available in the research community present an enormous opportunity for improving our ability to reduce mortality from cancer, improve therapies and meet the demanding individualization of care needs.

From an architectural point of view the ACGT environment is based on a layered architecture which contains two bottom layers representing the grid infrastructure. The lowest layer represents basic grid services providing remote access to physical resources. On top of that the second grid layer consists of more advanced grid services responsible for resource management, data management, and security.

That kind of Grid platform can be used by any other ACGT specific services dealing with bio-research.

S.C. Lin and E. Yen (eds.), *Production Grids in Asia: Applications, Developments and Global Ties*, DOI 10.1007/978-1-4419-0046-3_8,

The important thing is that all services come under unified authorization framework based on the commonly used Grid technologies.

In the paper there are two examples of how to use Grid environment in ACGT: oncosimulator - standalone application that requires a lot of computational power to simulate tumor growth. The second example is GridR tool - gridify version of well known R environment provides broad range of state-of-the-art statistical, graphical, and advanced data mining methods.

2 ACGT Architecture

The ACGT environment is based on a layered architecture (see Fig. 1).

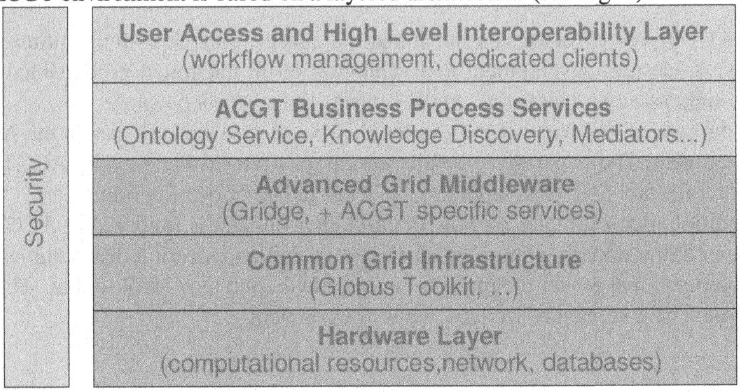

User Access and High Level Interoperability Layer
(workflow management, dedicated clients)

ACGT Business Process Services
(Ontology Service, Knowledge Discovery, Mediators...)

Advanced Grid Middleware
(Gridge, + ACGT specific services)

Common Grid Infrastructure
(Globus Toolkit, ...)

Hardware Layer
(computational resources,network, databases)

Security

Fig.1. Overall architecture of ACGT

The lowest level layer on the bottom of the ACGT system architecture is the Hardware Layer. It consists of physical resources scattered throughout Europe, connected using some network infrastructure. The two main types of resources are computational nodes and data nodes (storage system or databases). All resources from the Hardware Layer should be accessed remotely in an as much unified way as possible.

The Common Grid Infrastructure layer is responsible for providing mechanisms for remote access to resources in a "grid" way. It provides basic functionality required for remote computing and data access, like job execution and control, basic authentication and authorization, file transfer, database access, hardware monitoring, and information about state of resources (static and dynamic metrics).

The Advanced Middleware Layer is responsible for providing more advanced mechanisms in the grid environment. Services from this layer can be described as "collective" because they operate on a set of lower level services to realize more advanced actions, e.g., a meta-scheduling service that submits jobs to different local queuing systems using the Common Grid Infrastructure remote interfaces.

The functionality provided by this layer can be gathered in the following main points: resource management – meta-scheduling, data management (database access and file storing and transferring), services authorization, grid monitoring

As it can be seen on architecture picture the Grid layers are separated from the rest of the system that is build with services that provides specific ACGT content.

The advantage of it is clearly visible: based on that Grid platform it is possible to build many different environments for different fields, not only biomedicine.

Grid layers are supposed to provide standard and secure way for accessing hardware resources of the Grid environment.

On top of the grid layers there are two high level ACGT specific layers. The ACGT Business Process Services layer consists of components which are not aware of physical resources and single services in the grid environment. The grid is used as a whole to perform more abstract actions and to get information required by end user. Services of this layer use an abstract description of world defined as specific ontology.

There are also services that are able to translate a high level description to a language understandable by the lower layers (Grid). It provides higher level integration of different resources and data and makes them more similar to real word objects. The layer gathers all application and tools that provide access to the ACGT Environment for the end user. The most important component is ACGT portal, but there are also some specialized applications, i.e. for visualization purposes.

3   GRIDGE Technology

3.1   Overview

The Gridge Toolkit [2] is an open source software initiative which aims at helping users to deploy ready-to-use grid middleware services and to create productive grid infrastructures. All Gridge Toolkit software components have been integrated and form a consistent distributed system following the same interface specification rules, license, quality assurance and testing procedures. Gridge is a Grid-In-The-Box solution that can be easily deployed on a new infrastructure.

In detail, the Gridge tools and services enable applications to take advantage of a dynamically changing grid environment. These tools have ability to deliver dynamic or utility computing to both, the application users and developers and resource owners. Through supporting the shared, pooled and dynamically allocated resources and services, managed by the automated, policy-based Grid Resource Management System (GRMS) that interfaces with services as monitoring system, adaptive component services, data and replica management services and others, Gridge offers state of the art dynamic grid features to applications.

3.2   Resource Management

The component responsible for resource management within Gridge Toolkit is GRMS (Gridge Resource Management System). It is an open source meta-scheduling system, which allows developers to build and deploy resource management systems for large scale distributed computing infrastructures. GRMS is based on dynamic resource selection, mapping and an advanced scheduling methodology, combined with feedback control architecture, and deals with dynamic grid environment and resource management challenges, e.g., load-balancing among clusters, remote job control or file staging support. Therefore, the main goal of the GRMS is to manage the whole process of remote job submission to various batch queuing systems, clusters or resources. It has been designed as an independent core component for resource management processes which can take advantage of various low-level core services and existing technologies. Finally, GRMS can be considered as a robust system which provides abstraction of the complex grid infrastructure as well as a toolbox which helps to form and adapts to distributing computing environments.

GRMS is a central point for resource and job management activities and tightly cooperates with other services responsible for authorization, monitoring, and data management to fulfil the requirements of the applications. The main features of GRMS are job submission, job control (suspending, resuming, cancelling), the ability to chose "the best" resource for the job execution using multi-criteria matching algorithm, support for job check pointing and migration, support for file staging, storing information about the job execution, user notifications support, workflow jobs support etc.

GRMS has been designed as an independent set of components for the resource management processes which can take advantage of various low-level core services as, e.g., GRAM [3], GridFTP [3] and the Gridge Monitoring System, as well as various grid middleware services, e.g., the Gridge Authorization Service and the Gridge Data Management Service. All these services working together provide a consistent, adaptive and robust grid middleware layer which fits dynamically to many different distributing computing infrastructures. The GRMS implementation requires the Globus software [3] to be installed on the grid resources, and uses the following core Globus services deployed on the resources: GRAM, GridFTP, and MDS (optional). GRMS supports the Grid Security Infrastructure by providing GSI-enabled web service interfaces for all clients, e.g., portals or applications, and thus can be integrated with any other compliant grid middleware.

One of the main assumptions for GRMS is to perform remote job control and management in the way that satisfies users (job owners) and their applications requirements. All user requirements are expressed within an XML-based resource specification document and sent to GRMS as SOAP requests over GSI transport layer connections. Simultaneously, resource administrators (resource owners) have full control over owned resources on which the jobs and operations will be performed by an appropriate GRMS setup and installation. GRMS together with the core services reduces operational and integration costs for administrators by enabling grid deployment across heterogeneous (and maybe previously incompatible) cluster and resources. Technically speaking, GRMS is a persistent service within a Tomcat/Axis container. It is written completely in Java so it can be deployed on various platforms.

3.3   Data Management

Data storage, management and access in the Gridge environment are supported by the Gridge Data Management Suite (DMS). This suite, composed of several specialized components, allows building a distributed system of services capable of delivering mechanisms for seamless management of large amounts of data. It is based on the pattern of autonomic agents using the accessible network infrastructure for mutual communication. From the external applications point of view DMS is a virtual file system keeping the data organized in a tree-like structure. The main units of this structure are meta-directories, which allow creating a hierarchy over other objects and metafiles. Metafiles represent a logical view of data regardless of their physical storage location.

Data Management System consists of three logical layers: the Data Broker, which serves as the access interface to the DMS system and implements the brokering of storage resources, the Metadata Repository that keeps information about the data managed by the system, and the Data Container, which is responsible for the physical storage of data. In addition, DMS contains modules which extend its functionality to fulfil the enterprise requirements. These include the fully functional web based administrator interface and a Proxy to external scientific databases. The Proxy provides SOAP interface to the external databases, such as for example those provided by SRS (Sequence Retrieval System).

The Data Broker is designed as an access point to the data resources and data management services. A simple API of the Data Broker allows to easily access the functionality of the services and the stored data. The Data Broker acts as a mediator in the flow of all requests coming from external services, analyzes them and eventually passes to the relevant module. The DMS architecture assumes that multiple instances of the Data Broker can be deployed in the same environment, thus increasing the efficiency of data access from various points in the global Grid environment structure.

The Metadata Repository is the central element of the Gridge distributed data management solution. It is responsible for all metadata operations as well as their storage and maintenance. It manages metadata connected with the data files, their physical locations and transfer protocols that could be used to obtain them, with the access rights to the stored data and with the metadescriptions of the file contents. Currently each DMS installation must contain a single instance of the Metadata Repository, which acts as a central repository of the critical information about the metacatalogue structure, user data and security policy for the whole DMS installation.

The Data Container is a service specialized towards the management of physical data locations on the storage resources. The Data Container API is designed in a way to allow easy construction and participation in the distributed data management environment of storage containers for different storage environments. The Data Containers currently available in the DMS suite include a generic file system Data Container, a relational database Data Container and a tape archive Data Container. The data stored on the various storage resources can be accessed with one of the many available protocols including such as GASS, FTP and GridFTP.

The Proxy modules are services that join the functionality of the Metadata Repository allowing to list the available databanks, list their content, read the attached metadata attributes and to build and execute queries, and of the Data Container to provide the data using the selected data transfer protocol. Such Proxy container are highly customized towards the specific platform they are working with to allow building complex queries and executing operations on the found entries.

3.4 Security Services

The most important element of security infrastructure in Gridge is authorization service called GAS. The Gridge Authorization Service (GAS) is an authorization system which can be the standard decision point for all components of a system. Security policies for all system components are stored in GAS. Using these policies GAS can return an authorization decision upon the client request. GAS has been designed in such a way that it is easy to perform integration with external components and it is easy to manage security policies for complex systems. The possibility to integrate with the Globus Toolkit and many operating system components makes GAS an attractive solution for grid applications.

Generally, an authorization service can be used for returning an authorization decision upon the user request. The request has to be described by three attributes: user, object and operation. The requester simply asks if the specific user can perform the operation on the specific object. Obviously, the query to an authorization service can be more complex and the answer given by such service can be complicated, too. One of the services which can work in such scenario is the Gridge Authorization Service (GAS). GAS has been designed in a form which enables many possible applications. GAS can communicate in many ways with other components. By using the modular structure of GAS it is easy to write a completely new communication module. The GAS complex data structure can be used to model many abstract and real world objects and security policies for such objects. For example, GAS has been used for managing security policies: for many Virtual Organizations, for services (like Gridge Resource Management Service, Mobile Services and other) and for abstract objects like communicator conferences or computational centres. These and many other features give a possibility to integrate GAS with many existing solutions. Such integration can be very important, because it raises the security level of the existing solutions and makes it possible to use the newest security technologies.

The main goal of GAS is to provide a functionality that would be able to fulfil most authorization requirements of grid computing environments. GAS is designed as a trusted single logical point for defining security policy for complex grid infrastructures. As flexibility is the key requirement, it is to be able to implement various security scenarios, based on push or pull models, simultaneously. Secondly, GAS is considered as independent of specific technologies used at lower layers, and it should be fully usable in environments based on grid toolkits as well as other toolkits. The high level of flexibility is achieved mainly through the modular design of GAS and usage of a complex data structure which can model many scenarios and objects from the real world. It means that GAS can use many different ways for communication with external components and systems, use many security data models and hold security policy on different types of storage systems. These features make GAS attractive for many applications and solutions (not only for those related with grids). GAS has to be the trusted component of each system in which it is used and it brings about that the implementation of GAS was written in ANSI C. This choice makes GAS a very fast and stable component which uses not much CPU power and little amount of memory. The main problem of many authorization systems is their management. It is not easy to work with a complex system in a user-friendly way. Based on many experiences and the end user comments together with GAS, the GAS administration portlet (web application) is provided, which makes management as easy as possible. Flexibility of this solution gives users a full possibility of presenting only these security policies which are important for them.

4   Scenarios

4.1   Oncosimulator application submission.

Submitting of computationally intensive jobs in the Grid environment is the typical use-case. The best example of this use-case for ACGT project is Oncosimulator application submission.

The Oncosimulator is an advanced information system which is able to simulate the response of tumours and affected normal tissues to therapeutic schemes based on clinical, imaging, histopathologic and molecular data of a given cancer patient. It aims at optimizing cancer treatment on a patient-individualized basis by performing in silico (on the computer) experiments of candidate therapeutic schemes.

Described below scenario concerns not only simple submission of application, but also presents integration with visualization tools

The first step of the scenario is devoted to preparation input data for the computation.

Clinician needs to prepare MRI sets of slices of a Wilms tumour, concerning the tumour before chemotherapeutic treatment (with vincristine and dactinomycin).

Using specialized tools he/she also needs to delineate tumour contours on provided slices.

The user uploads all required files from his/her machine to the Gridge Data Management System using web portal client. The files are then managed by DMS and can be accessed by the user or other services acting on behalf of the user.

Then using specialized Oncosimulator portlet user defines parameters of simulation by filling proper fields of portal form. The interesting feature of the system is ability to define arguments of execution in a parameter seep manner. So with the one click multiple runs can take place with parameters from defined set with selected step. This feature is supported on grid resource management level.

Besides parameters, location where the output data will be stored must be provided. It is used by Visualization System for presenting the results of computation.

After 'submit' button is clicked description of job for Gridge Resource Management System is built and then submitted to the system. In this case job definition

(XML document) is a workflow that consists of set of tasks and dependencies between them.

Tasks description (task as a single execution of the application or script) has two parts: one describing execution (executable file, input parameters, environment variables, etc.) the second one comprises resource (hardware) requirements for task execution. Based on that requirements resource management system can take decision where to put the task for execution. In the executable definition references to data management system are used.

In our scenario at first simulation code is unpacked, compiled and executed. During the application runtime all data generated is transferred to visualization system location provided by the user.

After the simulation finished all the output data is also uploaded to the Data Management System.

Detailed view of the submitted workflow is presented on following picture:

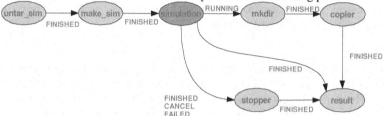

Fig.2.Workflow submitted to GRMS

Tasks on picture:
- untar_sim: unpacking of application code
- make_sim: compilation of the simulation code
- simulation: Oncosimulator simulation execution
- mkdir: task responsible for making directory for generated output by simulation on visualization machine
- copier: task responsible for transferring newly generated files to visualization site
- stopper: stopping the copier task as soon as the simulation stops working
- result: pack the output of the simulation and sends it to the Data Management System

After the job is submitted GRMS takes care about workflow management and provides additional information for monitoring purposes. User can take advantage of this information using the portal.

After the simulation finished all the output data is also uploaded to the FTP server of Visualization System and stored in Data Management System of the Grid.

4.2 GridR environment

In a previous contribution we have introduced GridR, showing how the R environment [4] can be used in a grid infrastructure. This section gives a detailed description of GridR according to [6] with main focus on grid-related aspects. GridR is based on the open-source statistical package R. The R environment provides a broad range of state-of-the-art statistical, graphical techniques and advanced data mining methods (including comprehensive packages for linear and non-linear modelling, cluster analysis, prediction, hypothesis tests, resembling, survival analysis, time-series analysis), it is easy extensible and turned out as the de facto standard for statistical research and many applied statistics project, especially in the biomedical field.

In the ACGT analysis environment, R is used as a user interface and as an analysis tool. R as user interface is supposed to serve as programming language interface to the ACGT environment. Used as analysis tool, the goal is to achieve a seamless integration of the functionality of R and the ACGT semantic data services in a grid environment, hiding complexity of the grid environment as the user might not want to or is not capable to deal with.

The client side part of the GridR toolkit is structured around the components "RemoteExecution" (JobSubmission and JobDescription Generator) and "Locking". The RemoteExecution component is responsible for the execution of R code as a job in the grid environment, using services provided by the grid layer of the ACGT architecture. It transforms the R code to be executed into a set of files, including the creating a job description file in the respective job description language, and submits it as job to a remote grid machine through an GRMS-client to the resource management system. During this process, the locking component takes care of the consistency of files/variables.

Accessing the ACGT grid environment requires no changes in the core R implementation. In practice, grid access is performed through the call of predefined R functions loaded from a package. R users can make use of the grid technology in a transparent way by passing the functions to be executed in the grid as input to one of those predefined functions (grid.apply) in their local code. The predefined functions build an R programming language interface that supports the access to the services of the ACGT environment. This means that R users and developers will have access to distributed resources in a transparent fashion, as if those resources were local. The complexity of the grid is thus hidden from the user.

The implementation of GridR was validated on the basis of the "Farmer scenario" [5], implementing some typical analysis steps of a microarray experiment. In the present case, R was used in conjunction with the BioConductor packages affy, affyPLM and marray, which are specialized packages for microarray analysis, to build the individual modules of validation.

Besides loading the expression data matrix and associated clinical data, those modules contribute in:

Producing some figures required for the quality control of the chips (e.g. RNA degradation plots)

Producing "MvA plots" to obtain an overall view of the fraction of differentially expressed genes.

Using a variance filter to pick unique probeset per gene and performing a principal component analysis, to verify that samples with similar subtypes group together.

Extracting symbols of genes most correlated to molecular markers relevant to the analysis (androgen receptor, AR, and estrogen receptor, ESR1).

The analysis steps are wrapped into functions for remote execution with GridR.

In the following the process of executing a single R function in the grid is described. The different steps of execution are briefly shown in Fig. 3

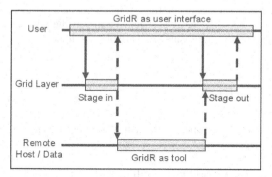

Fig.3. Steps of execution of R function in the Grid

1)   Library loading. The GridR functions are loaded from the GridR R package into the workspace of the R client.

2)   Grid initialization. The grid environment is initialized by calling the function grid.init. This function sets the paths to the cog-kit and the GRMS-client as well as the remote host that will be taken as execution machine.

3)   Code writing. The R code which is to be executed in the grid is written by the user and wrapped as single R function in the local R environment

4)   Grid submission. The grid.apply function is called, that launches the process of submission. At first, the function to be executed in the grid and the needed parameters are written into a file (fx.bin). Then the R script which is actually executed on the remote machine is generated (script.R), which is followed by the creation of the job description for the grid-job-submission by GRMS (job.xml). The job description file contains information for the resource management system, e.g. which application to execute in the grid (R in the present case), a dedicated execution machine, which files to stage-in (-out) from (to) the grid to (from) 'the execution machine etc. Next a shell file is created, which specifies the "workflow" which is performed on the client side (shell.sh). After that, the R client executes the created shell file in the background. That is, while the user can directly continue to work in the R session, the shell file creates a new proxy if necessary, performs the file copy from the client to the grid (to a GridFTP server later used for file stage-in), submits the job to the grid system and, after the execution is finished, performs the file copy of the result files (staged out by the grid system) back to the client machine. During the remote execution the created R script is executed on the remote machine, which reads the parameters and the function from fx.bin, executes $y=f(x)$ and writes the result into a file (y.dat).

5)   Waiting for result. While the remote execution is active and the R client waits for result (by checking if the file y.dat is created) the variable y is locked.

6)   Result processing. If file y.dat was created on the remote machine and, together with the result files, transferred back to the client, the file is loaded. The exit status is checked and – if the job was successful – the value is assigned to y and the variable is unlocked.

5   CONCLUSIONS

These two scenarios described in this paper are not the only ones that are developed in ACGT project.

The most advanced scenario that is still under heavy development is creation and execution of workflow. For this purposes, specialized workflow system was designed. It consists of two main components: workflow editor: tool for creation of workflows, and workflow enactor: BPEL compliant engine for workflow execution and control. This environment allows creating custom workflows of activities by the user and includes different components in it e.g. biomedical services invocation or fetching the data from various databases.

Grid services can also be part of workflow and used as a computational power provider, for advanced biomedical experiments.

The variety of different scenarios that includes the utilization of the grid confirms the design principles of ACGT architecture. The grid environment provided for the project is very flexible and covers a wide range of use-cases. It is worth to emphasize that all components of the ACGT architecture are designed and implemented with regards to the same, consistent security framework. It allows building a Virtual Organization and managing it in a dynamic way by defining access policies in an Authorization System.

Reference

[1] ACGT (EU): http://eu-acgt.org/
[2] Gridge Toolkit: http://www.gridge.org
[3] Globus Toolkit: http://www.globus.org
[4] R environment: http://www.r-project.org/
[5] P. Farmer, H. Bonnefoi, V. Becette, M. Tubiana-Hulin, P. Fumoleau, D. Larsimont, G. Macgrogan, J. Bergh, D. Cameron, D. Goldstein, S. Duss, AL. Nicoulaz, C. Brisken, M. Fiche, M., R. Iggo, ?Identification of molecular apocrine breast tumours by microarray analysis?, Oncogene, 24, pp. 4660-4671, 2005
[6] D. Wegener, T. Sengstag, S. Sfakianakis, S. Rping, A. Assi, ?GridR: An R-based grid-enabled tool for data analysis in ACGT clinico-genomics trials?, Proc. Of the 3rd IEEE International Conference on e-Science and Grid Computing, pp.228-234, 2007

Secure Grid Services for Cooperative Work in Medicine and Life Science

Anette Weisbecker & Jürgen Falkner

Fraunhofer Institute for Industrial Engineering, Nobelstr, Germany

Abstract

MediGRID provides a grid infrastructure to solve challenging problems in medical and life sciences by enhancing the productivity and by enabling location-independent, interdisciplinary collaboration. The usage of grid technology has enabled the development of new application and services for research in medical and life sciences. In order to enlarge the range of services and to get a broader range of users sustainable business models are needed. In Services@MediGRID methods for monitoring, accounting, and billing which fulfilled the high security demands within medicine and life sciences will be developed. Also different requirements of academic and industrial grid customers are considered in order to establish the sustainable business models for grid computing.

1 Introduction

In medical research and health care the requirements on the information technology (IT) increase. The progress in medical research and the complex integration of the supply chain in health care demand a powerful IT infrastructure. Grid technology provides a basis to fulfil these increasing requirements. Grid Computing enables the usage of hardware and software resources and furthermore, can support the secure collaboration between different institutions in the health care supply chain.

In the project MediGRID, a grid infrastructure has been built to solve challenging problems in medical and life sciences by enhancing the productivity and by enabling location-independent, interdisciplinary collaboration (Weisbecker, Falkner, Rienhoff 2007). The MediGRID project is part of the German D-Grid Initiative and is funded by the German Federal Ministry of Education and Research under the registration mark 01AK803A-01AK803H. MediGRID enables the usage of D-Grid resources for the medical community. It gives an easy, secure and transparent access to a broad spectrum of applications.

S.C. Lin and E. Yen (eds.), *Production Grids in Asia: Applications, Developments and Global Ties*, DOI 10.1007/978-1-4419-0046-3_9,
© Springer Science + Business Media, LLC 2010

MediGRID has selected three classes of applications to demonstrate the advantages of grid computing in medicine and the life sciences: In Biomedical informatics the connections between molecular data and biological phenomena or a clinical phenotype using computing is shown. The use of computing is an established part of biomedical data analysis. The enormous growth of knowledge through genome sequencing and systems biology will lead to growing numbers of in-silico experiments. These are ideal conditions for the use of grid computing. For medical image processing, the quality and quantity of image data are increasing exponentially. The use of tools and methods from grid computing will enable the users to solve scientific problems in medical image processing efficiently. The applications currently being tested are statistical analyses of large image data sets from functional nuclear magnetic resonance (fMNR), extensive hemodynamic simulations of virtual vascular surgery and complex analysis of clinical 3D ultrasound pictures of prostate biopsies. In clinical research the grid-based analysis of multi parametric data sampled from sleeping patients (polysomnography) requires the consolidation of data from a variety of sources. This requires high levels of data privacy and security for sensitive patient data.

MediGRID has shown the advantages of Grid Computing in medicine and life science. These are a substantial reduction of overall processing times and an easy-to-use access to applications together with a transparent access to various distributed information sources of academic and clinical providers. The usage of grid technology enables the development of new medical applications and services. The challenge is to define and provided secure grid services and business models for an on-demand usage.

As an advancement of MediGRID the project Services@MediGRID will define and implement grid services for medical research and health care accompanied by appropriate business models. As MediGRID Services@MediGRID is part of the German e-Science initiative D-Grid. The Services@MediGRID project is funded by the German Federal Ministry of Education and Research under the grant number 01G07015A-G.

2 Services@MediGRID – Vertical Grid Services for Biomedical Collective Research

The aim of Services@MediGRID is the implementation of sustainable business models to create an economically stable basis for existing MediGRID services and grid infrastructure. Relevant methods concerning monitoring, accounting, and billing must fulfill the high security demands within the scope of medicine and life sciences. Privacy regulations in medical research and health care specify highest demands concerning security, confidentiality, and availability of the data to be processed. Also the different requirements of academic and industrial grid customers have to be considered in order to establish the sustainable concept.

This applies to technical specifications and realization, as well as to transparent charge of usage of the grid infrastructure while the confidentiality of the data can still be guaranteed. Charging of services presumes billing metrics and service conditions, both reasonable and adjusted to the requirements of customers and providers. This implies a basis for a sustainable positioning of the platform and the services provided by MediGRID. Professional academic and industrial grid service providers offer grid services on commercial principals or integrate grid services of other grid service providers into their own product portfolio allowing themselves to provide these to their own customers. Services@MediGRID offers coaching by grid specialists to assist the embedded academic and industrial partners from the field of life sciences in using grid technology.

In order to establish a market for grid services in the medical and life science community industrial and academic partners work together. The different partners in Services@MediGrid and their application areas are:
- Collaborative Research Centre SFB 680 (University of Cologne):
  Moleculare Basis of Evolutionary Innovations
- University of Heidelberg, MoBiTec, Invitrogen:
  Molecular and cell biology, Genome Browser
- Bayer Technology Services:
  Identification of dynamic models of biological systems
- University of Kiel / c.a.r.u.s :
  volume oriented billing of genetic and high-throughput screening analysis
- Institute for Human Factors and Technology Management (IAT) University of Stuttgart, GWDG, University of Göttingen, Zuse Institute Berlin:
  grid services

3 Secure Access to Grid Services

To fulfill the security requirements in the medical and life science community a PKI (Public Key Infrastructure) based authentication and authorization has been implemented. To get access to the grid services in MediGRID as well as in Services@MediGRID, the users log on to the portal with their PKI certificates (Fig. 1). The implemented user management is based on a role-based virtual organisation management and uses a Virtual Organisations Management and Registry Service (VOMRS) provided by the German D-Grid Initiative.

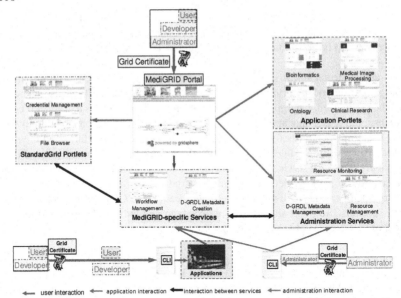

| ⬅️ user interaction | ⬅️ application interaction | ⬅️ interaction between services | ⬅️ administration interaction |

Fig. 1 PKI certificates based access to the services in MediGRID and Services@MediGRID

Three main roles in the virtual organisation management are distinguished:

- Users have access to the medical and biomedical application via the portal. The portal is implemented with the gridsphere framework. The applications user interfaces are provided in the portal by portlets.

  The implemented portal acts as the user entrance to the world-wide accessible grid services (applications) and resources. For each application exists a portlet that allows users to run them without any knowledge about the underlying grid architecture.

- The developer of the applications gets access to the development portlets. The developer defines the steps of the application process with workflows. Furthermore, the developers have to describe the characteristics of the application.

- Resource providers and administrators of central grid services use the administrations portlets.

  The administrators are responsible for the metadata management and the resource monitoring.

For the usage of the grid services two different access possibilities are available. First, the PKI based registration which guarantees the authentication and authorization of each user, and second, a guest user registration for applications with low security requirements for example biomedical ontologies (Fig. 2).

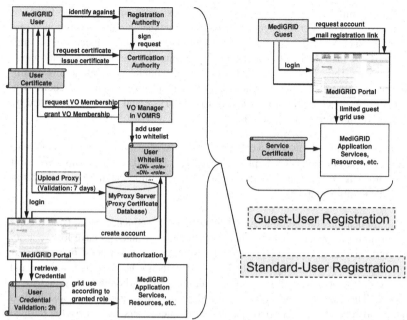

Fig. 2 PKI based registration for standard users and guest user registration

The standard MediGRID and Services@MediGRID user needs a certificate for the usage of services and the D-Grid resources. In order to get this certificate the user has to identify himself against a local trusted Registration Authority. Most companies which participate in D-Grid don't have an own Registration Authority. Therefore, they have to build one up. This is for most of the companies an obstacle because of the technical and organizational requirements.

After the user has identified himself against the Registration Authority, he needs to apply for a PKI certificate at a trusted Certification Authority. The Registration Authority signs the request. After the user received his certificate, he can install it in his browser.

In the next step the user registries at the Virtual Organisations Management and Registry Service (VOMRS). This service is provides by D-Grid. It checks the validity of the user certificate and if the certificate was issued from a trusted Certification Authority. After the user is identified, he can request for a membership in a virtual organization (VO) by registering himself at the requested VO. For a fine granular rights management different sub VOs according to the application classes in MediGRID and Services@MediGRID have been established. The subdivision into sub VOs provides a basis for a role-based access control within the grid in the future. During the registration process, the user gets an email registration link. This email contains the usage policy the user has to accept. After this the VO

Manager is informed by email of the users request and confirmed or declined the membership. If the VO Manager confirmed the membership the user is added to a whitelist. Each D-Grid resource uses the whitelist and makes a local user account which can be map on the globus grid map file. Thus the user has an operation system account. The MediGRID portal also use the whitelist to create automatically the user account at the portal. The user now has also a gridsphere account. The user can use the certificate to get access to the service and resources provided by MediGRID and Services@MediGRID.

In order to enable the user to work from everywhere, especially with a computer with is not part of the grid a myproxy upload tool is used. With this Java Webstart application the user get his certificate into the grid without having his computer in the grid (Krefting et al. 2008).

Some applications for example AUGUSTUS a DNA-sequence-based gene prediction program for eukaryotes, i.e. organisms with a cell nucleus have low security requirements but a lot of users world wide. For these users a guest registration is provided. The user can register to the portal with username, email address and password. The account will be activated automatically, when the email address is verified. The guest user gets a personalized account with guest status and limited rights and functionality. After registration, the guest users can access the defined services by logging on to the portal with their username and password. However, these services still need to use credentials for communication with and access to the grid resources. One possible solution of this problem is the approach of service certificates. The respective services use service certificates instead of user credentials. The provider of such a service needs a service certificate from a trusted Certification Authority for his service. The provider is therefore responsible for this service and its usage.

4   Role and Business Models for Grid Services

For the sustainable organisation of a grid infrastructure and the offering of grid services to industrial and academic customer's business models are needed. A business model implies of different views. According to (Scholz et al. 2007) a business model consists of five elements:
-   The utility view considers the overall strategic aspects and the value added by the services offered to the user.
-   The value creation view analyses the participants, structures and processes of the value chain.
-   The capital view focuses on the revenue model, costs and financing aspects.
-   The technological view shows the underlying grid architecture.

- In medicine and life science the legal and sector-specific restrictions have to be regarded, for example guidelines for security and data privacy.

By the definition of the service, the product which should be offered to a customer has the main focus. This includes the value proposition and the value of the service for the customer. For the derivation of the value proposition, the different roles involved by the creation, production, and usage of a service are important. Therefore, a role model has been defined in Service@MediGRID (Fig. 3). It describes the different roles of the involved partners. The structure of the role model is oriented on the grid architecture which builds the basis in MediGRID and Services@MediGRID (Weisbecker, Falkner, Rienhoff 2007).

The resource providers deliver hardware in form of compute resources, storage, network connections, data bases and devices. They provide and operate the resources.

The grid middleware providers make sure, that the different grid resources can communicate with each other. This can be providers of commercial grid middleware products, national or international grid initiatives or open source product supplier.

Based on the grid middleware a lot of infrastructure services are needed. These services are provides by infrastructure service providers. An example can be the D-Grid Initiative in German.

The application service providers supply the application in the area of medicine and life science. These includes in the applications classes of MediGRID like bioinformatics, medical image processing and clinical research as well as application classes from Services@MediGRID like high-throughput screening analysis, drug research and visualisation of results of the genome research. The application service providers are followed by the service providers. They provide not only software services but value added services which may comprise of applications, the compute power and consulting services. This can also include consulting services for the usage of an application. Additional services can be the consulting how application can be made running in a grid under consideration of technical and economical aspects. A further role accompanies the content providers. In medicine and life science, they provide for example research results or ontologies.

The customer organisation stands for the customer view and their requirements on grid services. This includes technical, organisational and economical aspects. A customer organisation must answer the question whether a service is provided by itself or brought from a service provider under consideration of all important aspects like reliability, security, costs.

A specific consideration is on the users. As members of the customer organisation the users need an easy and user friendly access to the grid services in order to fulfil their tasks.

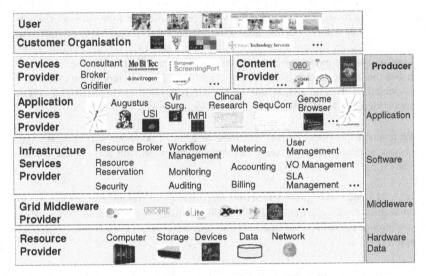

Fig. 3 Role model in Services@MediGRID

Based on this role model the next steps in Service@MediGRID are to define appropriate business models for the services which will be provided.

5 Conclusion

Grid computing and other models for providing resources like cloud computing, on demand computing or on demand applications change the way how organisations use compute resource. The goals of all these technologies is to provide better scalability of IT systems, enhancement of availability of IT services, increasing performance and reduction of costs. Therefore a clear definition of services with appropriate business models are needed in order to exploit the benefit of technologies like grid computing for industrial and academic customers.

References

[1] Krefting, D. et al. (2008). MediGrid – Towards a Towards a user friendly secured grid infra-structure. Article in Press. Future Generation Computer Systems. Amsterdam: Elsevier

[2] Scholz, S., Breitner, M. H., Semler, S. C., Blaurock, M. (2007). Business Models for grid computing in Life Sciences: An Approach to Identify Healthgrid Revenues. MEDNET 2007 12th World Congress on the Internet in medicine, 09.10.2007, Leipzig. http://mednet2007.com/content/news.php?item.58. Last Visit 10.10.2008.

[3] Weisbecker, A., Falkner, J., Rienhoff, O. (2007). MediGRID – Grid Computing for Medi-cine and Life Science. To appear in Lin, S. C., Yen, E. (Eds.). Grid Computing - Interna-tional Symposium on Grid Computing (ISGC 2007). Berlin, Heidelberg: Springer

From tools and services to e-Infrastructure for the Arts and Humanities

Tobias Blanke

Centre for e-Research/Arts and Humanities Data Service, King's College London, United Kingdom

Abstract

This paper presents tools and services, humanities researchers use to work with digital resources. It will then analyse how these tools and services can be brought together in one integrated research infrastructure empowered by e-Science tools and methodologies e-Science stands the development and deployment of a networked infrastructure and culture through which resources can be shared in secure environments. This networked infrastructure allows a culture of collaboration, in which new forms of collaboration can emerge, and new and advanced methodologies can be explored.

1. Introduction - Changing Research in Humanities

Research is changing, not only because the intellectual process is a dynamic activity anyway, but also more specifically due to the changes new digital resources bring about. In the last decades we have witnessed the development of large num resources can be shared in secure environments. These resources can be everything from processing power, data, or expertise that researchers can share. This networked infrastructure allows a culture of collaboration, in which new forms of collaboration can emerge, and new and advanced methodologies can be explored. In this paper we are first going to look at the tradition of computing and humanities. We will present the use of digital tools and methodologies in the humanities. Humanities have been using computers for their research almost since these have been invented. They are institutions all over the world working on advancing the agenda of digital humanities. We will introduce digital humanities in the next section. In section 3, we will look at how e-Science fits into this agenda. Afterwards, we will present how virtual research environments could work for the humanities, before in section 5 we finally give examples of early exemplary projects in humanities that bring together tools and services into integrated research infrastructures for humanities.bers of digital resources for research in the humanities [4].

S.C. Lin and E. Yen (eds.), *Production Grids in Asia: Applications, Developments and Global Ties*, DOI 10.1007/978-1-4419-0046-3_10,
© Springer Science + Business Media, LLC 2010

These require different research means from those that the traditional `analogue' approach required. It is just not satisfying for a user of digital resources to be confronted with them like records in a library. In the digital world, we expect the easiness of Google to find not only whole documents but exact information in them. Alongside these changes in the information retrieval activities, new technologies for networking and digital data capture have emerged [6]. New forms of scholarly communication are enforced by these technologies.

In this paper, we are going to investigate what these changes mean for humanities research. In particular, we are going to look at how e-Science technologies and methodologies are changing humanities research [2]. E-Science stands the development and deployment of a networked infrastructure and culture through which

2. *Digital Humanities*

The application of computing in the humanities has a longer tradition than many people are aware of. Computers have been used by humanities researchers since the 1950s, almost ever since they have been invented. Relatively early, humanities researchers realized that computers are symbol manipulating machines rather than pure calculators. As symbol manipulating machines, computers lend themselves to many traditional humanist activities such as text analysis. No humanist would ever doubt the profound impact modern electronic word processing had on humanities research. Only with modern word processing, it became possible to reassemble texts without having to rewrite them. As much as other researchers, humanists use e-mails to communicate and online catalogues of libraries made it much easier to find the required source of information like the latest monograph on early modern history in Britain. Bibliographic software has cut the time spent on finding and referencing literature dramatically. Next to these generic tools, specialised tools help perform very specific tasks like concordance analysis, and scanners and optical character recognition services have changed the access to primary resources in the humanities for ever [7].

Next to this everyday use of computers in the humanities, specialised research institutions have developed. In the UK, the Centre for Computing in the Humanities (CCH) at King's College London1 is an established and important institution for digital humanities. Digital Humanities can be compared to what is known as computational sciences in disciplines like chemistry, physics, etc. Digital Humanities is centrally concerned with the common methods and techniques for analysing source materials, tackling problems and communicating results in the humanities disciplines [7]. In this sense, e-Science activities in humanities are part of the tradition of Digital Humanities in general. However, there is a lot of work to be done to see humanities e-Science as a continuation of what Digital Humanities has striven to achieve in its 50 years history rather than as an opposite or independent movement. Text Encoding is a good example. It has been at the heart of Digital Humanities for a long time. It is widely used and at the same time of high theoretical impact. Contrary to other Digital Humanities activities, it is (already) recognized as a valid addition to humanities research in general by employing computational methods. Text (en-) coding in the humanities, however, has mainly been centred around markup. The Text Encoding Initiative (TEI) standard2, has been very successful as a way for humans to annotate texts and make them understandable to other humans. It remains to be seen whether the standard can have a similar impact for providing a metadata standard to exchange texts between computational agents. This however would be its main use case in more computationally oriented e-Science for humanities. It has been tried as a metadata exchange standard in the TextGrid project3 in Germany as well as in the MONK project4 in the US. But both of them used only a subset of the extensive TEI specification in order to achieve TEI based interoperability.

On the other hand, traditional humanities activities such as the creation of critical editions could benefit from the collaboration in research enabled by new infrastructures that e-Science promises to deliver. Collaboration will help the further analysis and interpretation by researchers. More radical improvements can secondly be expected from advanced e-Science technologies used in the preparation and preparatory analysis of the material under consideration. Further statistical analysis of texts - as we know it from many other application domains such as information retrieval or text mining - had before been limited as the necessary computing infrastructure to support such work did not exist or if it existed was not available for use by humanities researchers. According to early research in Humanities Computing, literacy analysis using computers [7], e.g., would hugely benefit from unlimited access to high-quality electronic texts and from the ability to redefine the statistical analysis on-the-fly. We will look at one example in the section 5.1 about emerging e-Infrastructures in humanities.

E-Science promises to provide the virtual infrastructure to realize storage solutions that can provide virtually unlimited access to text research resources and powerful computing equipment that supplies unlimited computing power on-demand. Furthermore, it promises integrated virtual research environments [3], which allow researchers to work with the provided data in one integrated environment. Such virtual research environments would lead to a humanities e-Wissenschaft, as analysed in the following section.

3. Humanities e-Wissenschaft Tools

E-Science in the arts and humanities makes the double claim that arts and humanities research can be advanced by scientific and advanced computing methods at the same time. This double claim has helped develop grass-roots activities in the

UK [2], which included collaboration of arts and humanities researchers with scientists and computing experts. In his 2008 keynote at the UK All Hands e-Science5, Greg Crane suggested to give up the current term e-Science in favour of e-Wissenschaft. This German description of science allows for a more inclusive view of the requirements and achievements of new network technologies, which would include humanities. The theme of the 2008 UK e-Science All Hands was to bridge the gap between e-Science and existing computational sciences. For the humanities, this gap describes the attempt to overcome the separation of humanities e-Science and more traditional Digital Humanities activities, which are focused on the critical online publication of source material using annotation technologies. This would mean to use the experience gained in Digital Humanities to build integrated research infrastructures for humanities.

In Digital Humanities, it has been suggested for a long time that a humanities research infrastructure should not only include access to digital resources, but tools and services, which would enable humanities research. Information access services and tools for the humanities community are difficult to define, as the humanist work is characterized by the work with unstructured information, mainly text and images. It is unclear how to deliver exactly those information to the humanist, he or she needs. In order to achieve this, we need to start with the humanities researchers' workflow, with the way they seek information and use it.

Humanities researchers working with digital resources are focussed on means to perform their workflow tasks most effectively, as they often involve an extensive amount of manual labour by the researcher [7]. These tasks include easily accessible overviews of information resources, integrated access to secondary information resources and digitisation services [7]. Essential components of the humanists' work space to realize their tasks include therefore access services to primary and secondary sources, text analysis and presentation services. Next to these services, tools for communication and collaboration will help humanist researchers engage with their main activity: the discussion of the meaning of primary sources. These activities are easy enough to describe but often very difficult to support effectively in an information environment that is based on network access. Imagine e.g., the medieval historian who would like to browse through a collection of high-resolution large digitisation images of manuscripts in order to analyse, e.g., degraded surfaces and reconstruct fading documents. These images can be several 100 MBs in size and traditional network technologies will fail to provide bandwidth to support the researcher with the ability to flip forth and back through the digitisation images without severe interruptions due to network delays and bandwidth problems. Then, there are many other non-textual resources such as oral interviews where it is not at all clear how to provide efficient information access to a single resource alone.

A humanist work bench will have to support reading and re-reading, analysis and re-analysis of given resources. It is therefore not surprising that many humanities scholars do not consider the computer an absolute essential work platform [7]. Even basic reading on the screen is still very difficult. Annotations are also still done better with paper and pencil, although the limitations of this approach are known to humanities scholars if they browse through their immense collection of notes in search for a particular reference or idea. Databases to support access to notes or text classification services are enjoying a wide uptake in the humanities [7].

The next section describes the requirements for a humanities virtual research environment to support the workflow of humanities using e-Wissenschaft tools and services.

4. Humanities Virtual Research Environments

Current Digital Humanities applications often lack an integrated approach to support the complete research life cycle in humanities. A virtual research environment would bring together several Digital Humanities applications into an integrated infrastructure to support the complete life cycle of humanities research. Current humanities research tools often support only simple access services for the data items they contain and are not integrated into larger research infrastructures. In order to make the e-Science agenda work in those research domains where the traditional research life cycle includes a lot of library work such as social sciences or arts and humanities, digital library services need to be part of e-Infrastructure services. This has been expressed in the ground- breaking article What is a Digital Library Anymore, Anyway by Carl Lagoze, Dean Krat, Sandy Payette and Susan Jesuroga [5]. In the article, the authors describe the challenges repositories and digital libraries in general face in the age of the 'Googlization' of knowledge, which has infected funding agencies. The suggestion is that Google and other search engines create the perception that digital libraries are just about easy information search and access. However, traditional library services included much more than just access to knowledge. They offered spaces to collaborate and targeted services for specific communities. The authors also describe first attempts in the US to realise such a deep network of information using a marriage of data grid and repositories technologies [5].

The challenge for the virtual research environment of the future will be to provide value-added services to targeted user communities, and to link in information that is semantically connected to the stored information. In the humanities community, this could be additional bibliographical information about an author or references to co-authors. Moreover, not only humanities would benefit by the easy reactivation of past knowledge. Digital archives need to be able to more easily transform their stored knowledge into active knowledge, as we have described in [1]. This can only be the case if they are able to map their archival data formats into formats actively used in research processes. There is great potential for supporting digital curation and preservation using data grid and semantic technologies. This is where the new European wide research infrastructure described in section 5.2 sets in. Recent developments in data grid technologies such as iRODS6 or the OGSA-DAI framework7 promise a better abstraction of the data layer from the information layer so that curation and preservation can focus on building complex webs of relationships between information items, which are necessary to keep information useful for current and future research in the humanities.

Recent development in data grid technologies and repositories not only allow for an unprecedented scale of information to be stored together but also for the flexible description of corresponding information units. Data management in e-Science on the other hand will benefit from knowledge in the digital library and repository community in how to build information network overlays to map relationships between data and information items in order to provide intelligent access to large-scale research data. E-Science data management will extend to new research domains such as humanities where the focus is less on petascale data but on complex relationships between individual data items. Using technologies for integrating and vitalising disparate data resources, will allow these disciplines to see the advantages of e-Science tools and methodologies and publish their data to the wider e-Science/e-Research community.

To come up with solutions for the challenge of building a usable virtual research environment for the humanities, is an urgent task in Europe - driven by the large digitisation programmes there. In ancient times, the library of Alexandria was supposed to contain 70% of the world's knowledge. It is the declared target of the European Commission to top this number, at least for European knowledge. The EU's digital libraries initiative European claims nothing less but total and sustainable access to heritage research records.8 It focuses on cultural heritage and scientific information. In such a gigantic endeavour, humanities play the role of an important mediator. After all, their scientific information is often focused on cultural heritage artefacts. The European Union demands from its member states more investment into digitisation and an accelerated and more consequent online presentation of cultural artefacts. In the next section we introduce three humanities e-Infrastructure examples that could provide first answers to the pressing need to build virtual research environments on the scale as the European project demands.

5. E-Infrastructure

In this section, three humanities e-Infrastructure projects are presented that could provide answers on how to integrate tools and services in virtual research environments for humanities research. First, a possible institutional involvement is suggested before we discuss a European project to provide arts and humanities research infrastructures on the large scale.

5.1 Institutional involvement

A more recent development in UK e-Science is the emergence of university-based e-Research institutions, such as the Oxford e-Research Centre9, or the Centre for e-Research at Kings College London (CeRch)10. These centres are called e-Research rather than e-Science institutions to open up towards academic domains such as the arts and humanities, which have not yet been served by developments in e-Science. CeRch is heavily involved in several attempts to establish building blocks of a future e-Infrastructure for arts and humanities research. Together with CCH and in the context of its task to build an e-Infrastructure for King's College London, it will work on at least two case studies on how to link digital humanities work to the National Grid Service.

5.1.1.   The first project called `High Throughput Computing for Humanities e-Research (HiTHeR)'11 attempts to advance the use of High Performance Computing in digital humanities. The Nineteenth Century Serials Edition (NCSE) corpus contains circa 430,000 articles that originally appeared in roughly 3,500 issues of six 19th Century periodicals. Published over a span of 84 years, materials within the corpus exist in numbered editions, and include supplements, wrapper materials and visual elements. Currently, the corpus is explored by means of a keyword classification, derived by a combination of manual and automated techniques. A key challenge in creating a digital system for managing such a corpus is to develop appropriate and innovative tools that will assist scholars in finding materials that support their research, while at the same time stimulating and enabling innovative approaches to the material. One goal would be to create a `semantic view' that would allow users of the resource to find information more intuitively. However, the advanced automated methods that could help to create such a semantic view require processing power that is currently not available to CCH researchers. CCH has implemented a simple document similarity index that would allow journals of similar contents to be represented next to each other. The program used the lingpipe12 software to calculate similarity measures (specifically, the TF/IDF similarity measure on character n-grams) for articles within the corpus. A test using 1,350 articles, requiring a total of 910,575 ($n * (n-1) / 2$) separate comparisons, was executed on a Mac Mini, which took 2 days to process 270 documents, that is to perform $270 * 1,349 = 364,230$ comparisons. Assuming the test set was representative, a complete set of comparisons for the corpus would take more than 1,000 years. CeRch will build a Campus Grid Toolkit13 based on CONDOR and a connection to the National Grid Service that will allow us reduce this time significantly.

5.1.2.   The second project called `Linking and Querying Ancient Texts (LaQUat)'14 concerns advanced data integration. A current CCH project is preparing a publication of the inscriptions from Cyrenaica and Tripolitania, Roman provinces in modern Libya, although the wider group is working with inscriptions from elsewhere around the Mediterranean, as well as with papyri.

The data resources produced by these projects include corpora of texts marked up using TEI, and in particular using EpiDoc, which is an implementation of TEI developed specifically for inscriptions. As part of the Integrating Digital Papyrology project, CCH researchers have been working with copies of the Heidelberg Gesamtverzeichnis der griechischen Papyrusurkunden gyptens (HGV), a database of papyrological metadata. This database contains general information on some 65,000 papyri, including bibliography, dates, and places (findspots, provenances), mostly from Roman Egypt and the environs. The proposed work will use the data integration platform OGSA-DAI to provide an integrated view of at least two databases (with different schemas) in the field of epigraphy and one database together with an XML collection in EpiDoc.

These are two good examples of how Digital Humanities university institutions can be involved in larger infrastructure projects in arts and humanities..

5.2. DARIAH

CeRch is also a lead partner in the European Union funded project DARIAH15. DARIAH stands for `Digital Research Infrastructure for the Arts and Humanities' and is funded to conceptualize and afterwards build a virtual bridge between different humanities and cultural heritage data resources in Europe. DARIAH has commenced work in September 2009. The project aims to improve access to the many arts and humanities resources locked away in archives, libraries and museums all over Europe. To form the initial digital infrastructure of DARIAH, data centres in France, Germany, the Netherlands and the United Kingdom joined forces. Since then the consortium has grown to 14 partners from 10 countries. The partners will work out in more detail the plans for the actual construction of DARIAH, including which national/European grid infrastructures it should use. In order to (at least partly) build a virtual bridge for European arts and humanities research data, DARIAH has identified several alternative but possibly complementary solutions. DARIAH will probably concentrate on a combination of the digital repository system Fedora16 together with iRODS17, the new data grid technology developed by SDSC, to support the flexible, distributed virtualised storage of les, which we will introduce in this subsection.

DARIAH will integrate pan-European humanities research data collections by using advanced grid and digital repository technologies. Formally managed digital repositories for research data can provide an effective means of managing the complexity encountered in the humanities in general, and will take on a central and pivotal role in the research lifecycle. The DARIAH infrastructure will be fundamentally distributed and will provide arts and humanities publishers and researchers alike with a secure and customizable environment within which to collaborate effectively and purposefully. DARIAH is currently funded as a preparatory project for 2 years, with the perspective of getting the support of national funding bodies to transform DARIAH into a service. Part of the 2-years preparatory phase, are two demonstrators to showcase that the envisioned technical architecture is viable. In this paper, we would like to focus on the `Fedora' demonstrator concentrating on collections at the University of Copenhagen, which contain a mixture of digitisation images together with transcriptions in the standard TEI format. The developed system will integrate the access, archiving, and organization of electronic resources and will permit the harvesting of metadata. It will be extensible to realise future applications with external services. In this sense, the central aim of the demonstrator will be the evaluation of DARIAH as a robust and flexible infrastructure that allows easy exchange of its components.

Most humanities data items like the ones at the University of Copenhagen are `write once, read many' files: First, they are centrally created. Then, they are made available to the wider research community via distributing them through the network. Often data items are closely related to other data items, e.g. the transcription of a digitised text and the digitised text itself. However, these two data items are not necessarily stored at the same location. The collections in Denmark, e.g., are closely related to reference collections in Berlin. The data architecture building blocks for DARIAH will therefore have to cover the easy exchange of file type data, the ability to create relationships between files in remote locations and flexible caching mechanism to deal with the exchange of large single data items like digitization images. Distributed file services for transparent remote file access and services must have equivalent access to data regardless of the data's physical location. Ancillary services for this function include transparent addressing, cached data, data replication, file locking, and file logging.

DARIAH will be built on top of the existing EGEE gLite infrastructure18, which supports mainly High Energy Physics (HEP) use cases: in a single experiment, large amounts of data are being produced that will then be distributed across the storage network for experiments to be run against them. This is analogous to the situation in humanities where resources like the Copenhagen collection are centrally created and then distributed. However, there is an important difference. Generally, in HEP experiments data is not preserved in its entirety for future use; the data and experimental setup changes too quickly. However, humanities data in general, tends to be kept in preservation environments for an indefinite period to support future reuse. A data infrastructure to support humanities research will therefore have to be able to easily incorporate existing archived research data. One challenge for an effective data platform for humanities research data is therefore the integration of existing preservation and research environments via grid data management systems. DARIAH promises to use iRODS to support archiving of data. An SRM-iRODS integration will be developed, by analogy with existing SRM-SRB integration19, providing access to iRODS storage with the standard SRM interface in EGEE. Experiments at the partner sides [1] have shown that the iRODS rule engine can be used as the basis for an active preservation environment that automatically reacts to preservation events like the ingestion of data or file format transformations and takes these away from the concern of the user. We will investigate whether iRODS can be made an archival system for a gLite-based e-Infrastructure.

In addition to managing digital resources at the le level, any Virtual Research Environment for arts and humanities research data will need to manage the complex structural and semantic components of the resources. This is not something that is supported to any great extent by the grid middleware, so we will integrate an additional component to support this. The Fedora digital repository software [2] offers us the necessary flexibility to manage data items and their complex relationships. Fedora allows for the abstraction from the physical existence of digital objects on servers. Several digital objects can be brought together into one abstract compound one and aggregations and can be associated with several heterogeneous metadata schemas. Abstract objects can be linked with semantic web technologies (as an RDF/OWL graph). The architecture of Fedora is essentially service-orientated, with all functionality being exposed as web services; in particular, all data and metadata stored within a Fedora object is made available via web services, facilitating integration of the software with other components in a service-orientated environment. One of the DARIAH partners is the Max Planck Society Digital Library in Germany. Together with partners, it is building the eSciDoc framework20, which are additional services to support the Fedora repository framework such as federated access management and search services.

DARIAH is one way to build a research infrastructure for the humanities. It uses grid technologies together with digital library technologies to deliver services to support the information needs of humanities researchers. It integrates many services useful for humanities research and will focus less on automation of processing but on providing an infrastructure to support the main activity of humanities researchers, the attempt to establish the meaning of textual and other human created resources.

6. Conclusion

We have seen in the presented descriptions of humanities research activities that they form a special case for the establishment of a research infrastructure. Humanities research has always been more closely linked to advances in library management than to general technological developments. Gutenberg's invention of the printing press allowed for the creation and distribution of large libraries of research results. Paper reference systems in libraries made it easier to find these research results. The next challenge will be to present researchers in the humanities not only with results from finished research project published in articles and books but with digital research data. This will be the beginning of a new way of doing empirical research in the humanities. More primary resources are available and access to them changes dramatically with the new digital revolution for research through e-Science tools and methodologies. For those of us working on providing access to these resources and persevering and curating them as useful research material, the challenge will be to do this in such a way that researchers are closely involved. In the last section we presented two ways of doing so: In the two projects CeRch works on together with CCH, the emphasis is on building local infrastructures in specific humanities research institutions. DARIAH is a research infrastructure that builds upon existing national infrastructures. It is embedded in existing communities of service providers and `only' connects these using the new e-Science tools and methodologies. It is not the attempt to create something new.

Arts and Humanities e-Science has never limited itself to more traditional ideas of e-Science, which link e-Science mostly to the application of certain advanced network technologies in supporting sciences. These technologies like the grid have their place but they might generate the impression that the solution is already there and only needs to find the right application and those willing to give the money. From our experience also in the wider world of e-Science, e-Science will fail if it deems itself as just an application of technologies. Rightfully, it will then be perceived as an invasion of some technology know-it-alls, which know the solution without knowing the problem. This perception might be even worse in arts and humanities. Their development and success was at least in the past seldom linked to advances in computing. Men and women are still vastly superior to machines when it comes to discussing history, analysing concepts or revolutionizing arts.

References

[1].   Tobias Blanke and Mark Hedges. Providing linked-up access to cultural heritage data. In ECDL 2008 Workshop on Information Access to Cultural Heritage, Aarhus, September 2008.

[2].   Tobias Blanke, Mark Hedges, and Stuart Dunn. E-science in the arts and humanities - from early experimentation to systematic investigation. In E-SCIENCE '07: Proceedings of the Third IEEE International Conference on e-Science and Grid Computing, Washington, DC, USA, 2007. IEEE Computer Society.

[3].   Stuart Dunn, Lorna Hughes, and Sheila Anderson. Virtual research environments in the arts and humanities. In Proceedings of the e-Science All Hands Meeting, Nottingham, September 2005.

[4].   Joost Kircz. E-based humanities and e-humanities on a surf platform. Technical report, SURF-DARE, 1. June 2004.

[5].   Carl Lagoze, Dean B. Krat, Sandy Payette, and Susan Jesuroga. What is a digital library anymore, anyway? D-Lib Magazine, (11), November 2005.

[6].   Michael Nentwich. Cyberscience. Research in the Age of the Internet. Austrian Academy of Science Press, Vienna, 2003.

[7].   Elaine G. Toms and Heather L O'Brien. Understanding the information and communication technology needs of the e-humanist. Journal of Documentation, (64), 2008.

Digital Library Storage using iRODS Data Grids

Mark Hedges², Tobias Blanke¹ ,& Adil Hasan²

² Centre for e-Research/Arts and Humanities Data Service, King's College London, United Kingdom

² Department of English, Liverpool University, United Kingdom

Abstract

Digital repository software provides a powerful and flexible infrastructure for managing and delivering complex digital resources and metadata. However, issues can arise in managing the very large, distributed data files that may constitute these resources. This paper describes an implementation approach that combines the Fedora digital repository software with a storage layer implemented as a data grid, using the iRODS middleware developed by DICE (Data Intensive Cyber Environments) as the successor to SRB. This approach allows us to use Fedoras flexible architecture to manage the structure of resources and to provide application-layer services to users. The grid-based storage layer provides efficient support for managing and processing the underlying distributed data objects, which may be very large (e.g. audio-visual material). The Rule Engine built into iRODS is used to integrate complex workflows at the data level that need not be visible to users, e.g. digital preservation functionality.

1. Introduction

Research across the academic disciplines is increasingly both driven by and a generator of data on a large scale, the so-called data deluge [3]. In the "big" sciences such as particle physics and astronomy, the primary emphasis has been the management of very large, petabyte-scale data sets, and the support of distributed access to such data, in particular by some form of data grid middleware. In other disciplines the emphasis is more on the complexity and richness of context of the data than on its numerical size. A digital resource need not consist of a single file or a simple collection of files, but may comprise a number of files of different formats with semantically tagged relationships between them. Moreover, researchers create assemblages of raw data, processed data, annotations, publications and other research outputs, which are themselves linked by complex relationships of provenance, and are linked to external data resources. Humanities researchers may use combinations of textual resources (enriched with various degrees of mark-up), long with databases and multi-media objects. Medical researchers may use large images with complex, detailed annotations. The complexity of the data is reflected in the complexity of the metadata that must be created and managed to support discovery and re-use of resources to an adequate degree.

Thus the curation of research material raises significant challenges that stem both from the amount of data that needs to be handled, and from its complex character. One approach to managing this complexity is to use some form of digital repository software. Digital repositories have for the most part been used to store relatively simple document-based digital objects, such as pre-prints, e-theses and e-books, where the forms taken and formats used are comparatively standard across academic disciplines. However, researchers are increasingly using such software to manage the complex and diverse digital material that is generated and used in academic research, and in particular for managing scientific data sets[6].

Nevertheless, while such systems facilitate the management of complex digital resources and their metadata, they are less well equipped to deal with issues of scale, physical distribution and persistence across time. With the growing internationalisation of any research discipline, data will often be stored at different locations that follow different storage solutions and management cultures. Users will require diverse, distributed digital objects to be integrated in a comprehensible form. Authorisation mechanisms must be able to provide a federated approach to managing access rights for users from various organisations. Requirements such as these cannot be dealt with in centralised information management architecture. In order to satisfy the needs of a highly diversified community, digital libraries need to look at virtualisation technologies that facilitate seamless resource-sharing and distributed accessibility.

The potential of digital library applications goes beyond the curation, discovery and delivery of data. As pointed out in [5], digital library systems can offer spaces for collaboration, and can incorporate services targeted at specific communities, as part of an integrated and extensive e-research infrastructure that supports the complete research life cycle. Users of such enhanced digital library systems may require specialised display, visualisation and processing, in many cases specific to particular categories of object, to be integrated into the system. But more flexibility will be required if it is desired to support a highly diversified community of users, such as the arts and humanities research community; it will not be possible to determine all the needs of such a community in advance, and the infrastructure will have to provide the means for researchers to create their own workspace within the infrastructure, where they can user their own services to process data curated by the digital library.

Providing access to research data in a virtual storage is only part of solution for a working digital library in research infrastructures. It is equally important to deliver services to clients that can be used for analysing and working with the information resources. We present in this paper our ideas of how virtual workspaces can be embedded in digital libraries for arts and humanities research using a combination of virtualisation services. A virtual workspace offers users of digital library services an execution environment that is made dynamically available close to the information resources in the digital library. This has two advantages for the client application. Firstly, it is often more efficient to run the code close to the data rather than transferring the data. Network traffic is reduced and possible scalability limits are overcome. Secondly, and this is even more important in research domains which deal with potentially sensitive data such as the medical and social sciences, but also the humanities, the data can stay at its original location, its licensed environment.

In this paper, we report on our experiences with a prototype architecture for supporting research in the arts and humanities, based on the Fedora digital repository software and the iRODS (Rule-Oriented Data management System) data grid middleware, developed by DICE (Data Intensive Cyber Environments) as the successor to SRB (Storage Resource Broker). The initial work was carried out at the Arts and Humanities Data Service (AHDS), in collaboration with the data grid services team at the Science and Technology Facilities Council4. The work is being continued by the Centre for e-Research at King's College London, which incorporated the Executive part of the AHDS in April 2008, when funding for the AHDS ceased.

2   Background: the AHDS and CeRch

The AHDS[5] was a UK national service with a remit that included the collection, management, preservation and dissemination of digital resources produced by research in the arts and humanities, and promoting the use of these resources in research and education. The structure of the AHDS was essentially distributed, comprising five Subject Centres, which specialised in particular disciplines, and a Managing Executive. Its collection policy was quite inclusive, accepting resources of great diversity, in terms of both discipline and format, and complexity.

From the start of April 2008, the AHDS was no longer funded to provide a national service. However, the AHDS Executive, which was hosted at King's College London, was incorporated into the newly created Centre for e-Research (CeRch)[6] at King's. CeRch is continuing the projects and research activities of the AHDS, although its remit now covers other disciplines in addition to the arts and humanities. As the curation of digital resources was a key service of the AHDS, the development of an appropriate digital repository infrastructure, capable of supporting these complex and diverse collections, was a central activity of the technical team. This is also a key area of interest for CeRch, and this paper describes some of the work that the AHDS/CeRch carried out in this area.

3   Initial Approach: Fedora and SRB

After a review of the available options, the Fedora7 digital repository software was selected as the most appropriate choice to support the AHDS' requirements for managing its digital assets. Fedora's architecture provides a highly promising model for managing the complex digital material with which researchers in arts and humanities disciplines have to deal. It has a very flexible "content model" architecture that supports the representation of compound digital resources and aggregations of in principle arbitrary complexity, and allows multiple heterogeneous metadata schemas to be associated with an object. It contains built-in support for semantically representing the internal structure of digital resources and contextual relationships with other resources, in the form of OWL/RDF graphs. The architecture is highly interoperable, with a service-orientated, standards-based approach, with all functionality being exposed as web services; in particular, all data and metadata stored within a Fedora object is made available via web services.

While the architecture is excellent for managing the complexity of digital resources, and for integrating with higher-level services, we have encountered issues at the data storage level, arising both from the increasing total size of the collections, and the potential size of individual objects. Although the data sizes managed at the AHDS were not large in comparison to those in the physical sciences, file size is increasingly an issue, for example in high-resolution digitisations of audiovisual material, manuscripts and works of art produced for use by scholars. Large data is also increasingly an issue in archaeology, a humanities discipline that frequently employs more "scientific" methods such as high-resolution 3D scanning [1]. This has become more of an issue as the Centre's remit has extended to other subjects within our host institution, for example biomedical researchers who generate very large files containing images and MRI scans.

However, if Fedora is to manage the data objects then they have to be held on a locally accessible filesystem[8], which does not result in a very flexible or scalable storage system. A preferable approach would be some form of distributed, virtualised storage. Such an architecture would also correspond better to the geographically distributed nature of the AHDS.

It was also noticeable that performance could deteriorate significantly when putting or getting very large objects into/out of Fedora. Digital objects in a Fedora repository are made available via web services, which can then be manipulated externally, e.g. by passing the data content to other web services or workflow tools; however, for very large objects this may be somewhat inefficient. Moreover, in some applications large digital objects were being transferred unnecessarily. Additional functionality may be implemented using Fedora's disseminator architecture, where disseminators are special objects that bind data streams in a Fedora object to elements in a WSDL file defining a web service, which is typically external to

Fedora. In one example, this mechanism was being used to display and annotate part of an audio-visual object, and the entire file was being transferred from storage to the Fedora application, and then delivered to the workflow, whereas only a small part of the object was actually relevant to the work being carried out. It would be possible to improve performance greatly in such cases if data transfer could be reduced and/or processing carried out locally to the data.

Moreover, part of the remit of the AHDS was digital preservation, and Fedora did not in itself provide the required services. Some experiments were carried out implementing such functionality using web-service orchestration, and the application layer. However, we considered that some preservation functionality is more appropriately carried out "under the hood" at the storage layer.

Data grid middleware, such as Storage Resource Broker (SRB), has been widely and successfully used for storing and managing large data objects and distributed data sets, and these systems provide support for such features as replica management, so that multiple copies can be maintained as insurance against corruption or loss. Work was already being carried out elsewhere on using grid storage for digital library systems, for example the DART project[9], which integrated Fedora with SRB, and the University of California, San Diego, which was integrating DSpace with SRB9. The initial pilot architecture for the AHDS used Fedora to manage the structure and semantics of the data and its metadata, and SRB to implement distributed storage and data management at the data level, using the existing Fedora-SRB plug-in.

4   Pilot Architecture: Fedora and iRODS

4.1   iRODS and Event-driven Rule Execution

The iRODS (Rule-Oriented Data management System) [7] is an open source project being developed by the San Diego Supercomputer Centre (SDSC) as the successor to Storage Resource Broker (SRB) [2], which has been widely used for implementing virtualised storage and data grid systems. Although iRODS is based on the experience gained from SRB, its functionality is significantly enhanced.

A particular feature of iRODS is the ability to represent data management policies in terms of rules. The system incorporates a Rule Engine, which interprets these rules and allows pre-defined sequences of actions (represented as "microservices") to be executed in particular circumstances. Rule execution results in the creation of persistent state information, which can be accessed from within rules to track and control subsequent rule execution.

One way of using rules is to allow users to invoke them explicitly, via the command and API interfaces provided, allowing specific data processing to be rules, which are executed automatically by iRODS as part of its normal execution, independently of any external request, in response to certain conditions or triggers. These rules have great potential for implementing data management strategies that are to take place "under the hood", where the data owners need to be confident that certain processing is occurring, but do not want to concern themselves with it. In particular, it is possible to define sets of rules for execution when an object is put into or retrieved from an iRODS grid, or when such an object is updated, and these rules can be executed either pre- or post- the action in question. Moreover, rules can be configured for execution at periodic intervals.

The iRODS system thus addresses two particular limitations of the SRB. In an SRB grid, it was possible to execute code implementing specific application requirements only by making changes to the core code, by implementing the functionality within external clients interacting with the SRB system via the SRB API, or by using SRB proxy commands to invoke executables on the SRB server10. The iRODS system provides a simpler, more flexible and integrated means of implementing such requirements within rules.

Another limitation of the SRB was its relatively restricted support for metadata extensions. Although SRB can incorporate user-defined metadata, this must be either in the form of attribute-value pairs, or else in additional tables that are held centrally within the MCAT database and can be queried using an SQL-like syntax. It does not support directly the complex metadata required for curation and preservation without extensive coding effort. It is possible to access external metadata systems using the SRB proxy commands mentioned above. However, an advantage of the iRODS rule system is that it provides a simpler and more integrated mechanism for access to external systems supporting more complex metadata management, for example, digital repository systems holding complex, heterogeneous metadata about digital objects, or triple stores managing semantically-tagged relationships between objects.

Micro-services can make use of specialized processing provided by external systems and libraries, so long as these expose appropriate APIs; in other cases, where a suitable API is not available, it may be possible to implement web service interfaces though which the systems can be invoked. An additional enhancement to this would be to use a web service registry (for example, based on UDDI) allowing external services to be added, discovered and invoked dynamically. The use of external services does however raise issues of robustness that would require additional coding effort, for example if a call were made to an external system that was not running.

At one level, these rules resemble workflows created using a language such as BPEL, which can be used to orchestrate sequences of web services encapsulating atomic actions with mutual dependencies (although iRODS micro-services are not themselves web services, but are implemented as C functions with a standardized interface). However, there is a conceptual difference. BPEL is used to construct workflows representing business processes (in a very general sense of "business") from a participant-centric point of view. iRODS rules are more analogous to the "event-condition-action" (ECA) model found in an active database management systems, where actions are executed automatically at a data level when certain events occur. ECA as it is currently implemented in database triggers and stored procedures will move some program logic into the database itself, so that the database does cleanup operations and responds to events without the need for a separate application. ECA definitions consist of a set of rules, where the event component specifies what has to occur and the condition component specifies a logical test that, if true, fires the action part.

4.2   Defining a rule in iRODS

Firstly, let us briefly examine how an iRODS rule is defined [11]:

actionDef jconditionjwork°ow-chainjrecovery-chain

where *actionDef* is the identifier of the rule, *condition* defines the circumstances under which the rule will be invoked, *workflow-chain* is the sequence of actions that the rule will execute (separated by ##), and *recovery-chain* is the sequence of actions to be executed in case a failure occurs within *workflow-chain* (that is, it defines how a partially executed rule will be rolled back). The actions in a *workflow-chain* can be either micro-services or rules, thus a rule can be built up recursively from other rules. The ability to recover from partially executed rules is an important feature; however, in most of the examples given below, the *recovery-chain* will be omitted to improve clarity.

Information can be passed to rules, and between actions and micro-services within rules, by means of parameters, which can define either inputs or outputs. Information can also be shared between micro-services by writing to and reading from the *RuleExecInfo* structure, which functions as a blackboard for rule execution. Micro-services can also access data held within the iCAT metadata catalogue, which is the iRODS equivalent of SRB's MCAT.

5   *Application of Rules for Data Management and Processing*

The iRODS Rule Engine provides a simple and flexible mechanism for deploying and executing software that implements application-specific functionality within an iRODS data grid. In the planned architecture, we are using rules to implement a variety of functionality within the digital library. In this paper, we briefly describe two examples of rule applications:

- implementation of digital curation and preservation strategies;
- manipulation of digital objects to provide additional value to users.

5.1   Rules for Digital Preservation

Digital preservation may be described as the set of activities that are necessary to ensure continued access to digital objects as the technical environment changes, and there are two broad approaches: either the objects are modified so that they function in the new environment (format normalisation and migration), or the new environment is modified so that it can replicate the behaviour of obsolete file formats and software (emulation) [8].

The AHDS followed a migration-based approach, described in a set of Preservation Handbooks and Ingest Manuals12, which involved converting digital objects to one of a set of standard formats on ingested (format normalisation), with subsequent format migrations throughout the object life-cycle as formats or software become obsolete. The policies and procedures that form the basis of this representation are derived from the Preservation Handbooks and Ingest Manuals created by the AHDS, which between 1996 and 2008 built up a considerable body of knowledge and experience in the curation of the complex and diverse digital material produced by research projects in the arts and humanities and by digitisation programmes[13] .

However, while these procedures were invisible to the creators of the digital resources, they involved a great deal of complex activity on the part of the archive staff, which was becoming increasingly difficult to support as the amount of deposited material increased. The iRODS Rule Engine provides a mechanism for (partially) automating these procedures.

For example, on ingest a digital resource undergoes reviews and validation at various levels to ensure its quality and authenticity, such as scanning for viruses, checking file fixity and integrity, and checking that the format of a file is what it purports to be. Once the ⁻les making up the resource have satisfied these checks, they are prepared for ingestion into the preservation archive. This may involve converting the individual ⁻les making up the deposit into open formats more suitable for long-term preservation. In addition, it is necessary to create preservation metadata, which is information that supports and documents the preservation of digital content over time.

The processing undergone by an individual ⁻le within such a digital resource may be represented schematically by the following iRODS rule:
acPostProcForPut | |
 acCheckObjectIntegrity##acAnalyseObject##
acNormaliseObject##msiSysReplDataObj(PresRescGrp,all) |
nop##nop##nop##msiCleanUpReplicas

where *acPostProcForPut* is an action automatically executed after a file is put (using the iRODS *iput* command or API) into an iRODS grid, and *nop* means that no *recovery-chain* component is required for the corresponding component of the *work°ow-chain*. These component actions may be further broken down as follows:

```
acCheckObjectIntegrityjj
acVerifyChecksum##acScanForViruses |
 nop##nop
acAnalyseObject | |
acIdentifyObjFormat##acValidateObj##
acGenerateObjMetadata |
nop##nop##msiCleanUpObjMetadata
acNormaliseObject | |
acPerformNormalisation##acValidateNormalisation##
acGenerateObjMetadata | msiCleanUpNor-
mObj##nop##msiCleanUpObjMetadata
```

These actions in turn can be broken down until the base components of each *work-flow-chain* are micro-services.

The flexibility of the rule system allows much more complex scenarios to be implemented. For example, the ability to specify pre-conditions for rule execution may be used to execute different rules for different ⁻le formats or for other categorisations of digital objects. Furthermore, format conversion tools are unlikely to perform perfectly in all cases; indeed, something is lost in most conversions, and one of the aims of normalisation is to maintain those properties deemed significant in. In practice it may be necessary to execute a several tools before an acceptable result is achieved. This can be automated by exploiting another feature of iRODS rules - the ability to specify several rule definitions corresponding to the same goal, which can be executed in turn until one is successful, unsuccessful rule executions being rolled back to ensure that the system remains in a consistent state.

This work is described in more detail in [4].

5.2   Rules for Manipulating Digital Objects

The envisaged digital library environment will incorporate a panoply of tools to aid the researcher by adding value to the core objects deposited, and in many cases, this processing can take place automatically without user intervention[14]; scenarios may include the application of tools when a digital object is ingested, or conversely the automated processing of a set of digital objects when a new tool is incorporated or an old tool updated. Examples are the application of metadata extraction or text mining software to text-based resources, or the pre-processing of high resolution image files into collections of tiles at different resolutions to improve performance of image viewers [15]. The details of the processing required will vary for different categories of object, and these different processing scenarios can be represented as sets of rules that are triggered when particular events occur, using the mechanism described in Section 5.1.

In other scenarios, a researcher may want to apply a tool to a digital object, whether because the combination of object and tool is not configured in the rule base, or because the tool in question is not part of the standard installation, and needs to be "sent" to the data. These scenarios raise issues of how to link remote execution with the processing architecture of the chosen front-end (in our case Fedora), and how to ensure that the target environment is appropriate for executing code that has been developed in a potentially different client environment.

A final example, more closely linked to the Fedora architecture, concerns the integration of rule executions local to the data with the Fedora disseminator architecture, as a potential approach to the performance issues described in Section 3, where degradation in performance was observed due to the transfer of very large objects. In the example given, instead of transferring the entirety of a large video file and passing it to a service to be exerted and annotated, some or all of this processing can be carried out locally to the data when the object is requested or the Fedora disseminator id invoked. Such a mechanism will be all the more useful once researchers start to use digital libraries that are embedded in a wider infrastructure of data and services, rather than as stand-alone systems for searching and browsing.

6   Conclusion

In this paper we have outlined a prototype digital library architecture incorporating an iRODS-based data grid system that provides virtual, distributed storage, analogous to earlier systems that used iRODS' predecessor SRB. Not only does iRODS provide the storage layer, however, it incorporates a Rule Engine that provides a flexible mechanism for implementing a variety of complex processing that can be executed "close" to the data. The required processing may be represented as rules that are triggered automatically when certain events occur, for example when an object is ingested. As these rules can be implemented conditionally, iRODS implements the full event-condition-action model known from active database management systems. This provides a great degree of flexibility for implementing automated processing at the level of the storage layer, and we have experimented by implementing a number of data management requirements. We also investigated the use of the rule system for triggering software to support researchers in the manipulation of their data.

Our initial experiments, which are briefly described in the preceding sections, have demonstrated the feasibility of using an iRODS-based system as a combined storage layer and rule engine in our digital library architecture. With the success of these initial investigations, we were encouraged to begin a deeper analysis of the requirements for using iRODS, both for archivists who want to implement preservation services, and for researchers who want digital library environments to integrate tools and services that support them inn their research. During the first phase of this analysis, we are developing a more extensive set of iRODS rules that better reflect the complexity and context dependency of the arts and humanities resources that we curate. The final system will therefore incorporate virtualised storage on a data grid, a digital repository with enhanced metadata management facilities, and integrated functionality provided by specialised tools.

References

[1]   Tony Austin and Jenny Mitcham. Preservation and Management Strategies for Exceptionally Large Data Formats: 'Big Data'. Technical report, English Heritage Project No: 3984. September 2007.

[2]   C. Baru, R. Moore, A. Rajasekar and M. Wan. The SDSC Storage Resource Broker. In Proc. CASCON'98 Conference, Toronto, Canada, Nov.30-Dec.3, 1998.

[3]   Tony Hey and Ann Trefethen. The data deluge: an e-Science perspective? In F. Berman, A. Hey, G. Fox (eds.), Grid Computing: Making the Global Infrastructure a Reality, John Wiley and Sons, Hoboken, NJ, 2003

[4]   Mark Hedges, Tobias Blanke and Adil Hasan. Rule-based curation and preservation of data: A data grid approach using iRODS. Future Generation Computer Systems, (25), 2009.

[5]   Carl Lagoze, Dean B. KraRt, Sandy Payette and Susan Jesuroga. What is a Digital Library Anymore, Anyway? D-Lib Magazine, (11), November 2005.

[6]   E. Lyon. Dealing with Data: Roles, Rights, Responsibilities and Relationships. Technical report, Bath, UK, June 2007.

[7]   A. Rajasekar, M. Wan, R. Moore and W. Schroeder. A Prototype Rule-based Distributed Data Management System. In HPDC workshop on "Next Generation Distributed Data Management", Paris, France, May 2006.

[8]   K. Thibodeau. Overview of Technological Approaches to Digital Preservation and Challenges in Coming Years. In Proceedings of The State of Digital Preservation: An International Perspective, Washington DC, USA, 2002.

[9]   Andrew Treloar. Storage and Interoperability Work Package 2: Improve interoperability between Storage Resource Broker (SRB). based environments and Fedora Technical report, DART, 1. June 2007.

Architectural Design for GRID Clearinghouse Service

Johannes K. Chiang & Kiekang Chao

Dept. of MIS, National Cheng-Chi University, Taiwan

Abstract

Grid Computing provides advanced feature for computer resource sharing, distribution over the Internet. Large-scale collaboration and engineering development for GRID Computing has been initiated around the world. The vigorous momentum of the technology capture business attention. The resources management in such large-scale distributed environment becomes a great challenge, and will be the critical concern before GRID deployed into production operation while resource allocation and use need to be properly managed in realistic and economic justification.

This study aims to elaborate a new business model regarding service trading and billing. The Grid Architecture for Computational Economy (GRACE) framework can be the fundamental framework which reveals resource trading behavior. This paper explored the resource trading models and the way to integrate them into a uniform computing environment. Thereby the concepts and Architecture is to be investigated and extended with Economic Service Architecture (ESA). Last but not least, this paper carries out necessary Service Interfaces and Service Data Entities.

Keywords: Grid Services, Economic Model, Chargeable Grid Service (CGS), Grid Payment System (GPS)

1. Introduction

With the advance of new Internet technologies and with an increasing number of potential users, software and hardware firms face new challenges in ultra-performance and scalability design of computing systems. Grid computing, as one of the emerging technologies, brought the new approach of computing technology and evolved new paradigm of computing services.

In this sense, Grid Technology enables the virtualization of distributed computing and data resources such as processing, network bandwidth and storage capacity to create a single system image, granting users and applications seamless access to

S.C. Lin and E. Yen (eds.), *Production Grids in Asia: Applications, Developments and Global Ties*, DOI 10.1007/978-1-4419-0046-3_12,
© Springer Science + Business Media, LLC 2010

vast IT capabilities. Just as an Internet user views a unified instance of content via the Web, a grid user essentially sees a single, large virtual computer (IBM Grid Computing, 2004).

One of the ambitious cases on Grid Computing is Oxford University's Centre for Computational Drug Discovery's project that utilizes more than one million PCs to look for a cancer cure. Participants donate a few CPU cycles from their PCs through "screensaver time." The project eventually will analyze 3.5 billion molecules for cancer-fighting potential. More than 50,000 years of CPU power (based on a 1.5 gigahertz chip) have been put to work so far.

Institutions nationally and worldwide are using the Grid to conduct large simulations, analyze data and coordinate experiments in disciplines that require high-end computing resources, databases or equipment at widely distributed locations. The scientific and business community accessing these resources also will be highly distributed, often worldwide.

The resources in the Grid are heterogeneous and geographically distributed. Availability, usage and cost policies vary depending on the particular user, time, priorities and goals. Resource sharing has inevitably become an appropriate approach to leverage computing resources largely existed in different regions and various research institutions. Nevertheless, without economic considerations and mechanisms, Grid services, with whichever good intention to facilitate collaboration and resource sharing, could not find their place in real-life applications.

This research is thus meant to work out a distributed computational economy framework as an effective metaphor for the management of resources and application scheduling. For this purpose, we elaborate the potential economic-based Grid Clearinghouse service for wide-area parallel and distributed computing.

The Service Framework as well as the economic consideration will be further investigated and extended on the basis of the Economic Services Architecture (ESA) from OGSA. Last but not least, necessary mechanisms such as CGS, GPS, Service Data Entity and interface etc. will be carried out.

2. Grid Computing Technology and Economic-based Grid Resource Management

Grid computing allows geographically distributed organizations to share applications, data and computing resources. Being a new model of computing, GRIDs are clusters of servers joined together over the Internet, using protocols provided by the open source community and other open technologies, including Linux. Grid protocols are designed to allow companies to work more closely and more efficiently with colleagues, partners, and suppliers through:

Resource aggregation, allowing corporate users to treat a company's entire IT infrastructure as one computer through more efficient management.

Grid and Peer-to-Peer computing platforms enable the services regarding sharing, selection and aggregation of geographically distributed heterogeneous resources for solving large-scale problems in science, engineering, and commerce.

Database sharing allows companies to access remote databases. This is particularly useful in the life sciences community, where researchers need to work with large volumes biological data from a variety of sources. Engineering and financial firms also could benefit significantly. Collaboration is in its nature to enhance widely dispersed organizations to work together on a project with the ability to share everything from engineering blueprints to software applications.

The move toward providing IT services as a utility, similar to the telephone and power, has begun to emerge. While application service providers (ASPs) were probably the first harbinger of this emerging service, computing utility offerings are beginning to populate the landscape of offerings and those competitors, application infrastructure providers (AIPs) have launched utility-based IT offerings.

This move to computing utility is expected over a long period of time to ultimately supplant the traditional outsourcing model in which the services providers manage customer-owned infrastructures and generally take control of the customer's IT and network staff. On a worldwide level, the USA is the most advanced regions for this future generation of IT computing, followed by Europe and then Asia/Pacific.

The implications of this model will be felt across not just the IT industry but also across the telecommunications, hardware, software, and other IT services sectors. Hereby SOA may be the famous product aroused within the evolution. Thus, the impact of Grid computing is moving from technological aspect to business aspect. The economic value of Grid computing is captured significant high-tech business attention. The value should be evaluated through economic measurement and justification.

However, resource management and scheduling in these environments is a complex task. The geographic distribution of resources owned by different organizations with different usage policies, cost models and varying load and availability patterns is problematic. The producers (resource owners) and consumers (resource users) have different goals, objectives, strategies, and requirements.

To address these challenges of resource management, this paper applies Grid Architecture for Computational Economy (GRACE) framework (Rajkumar Buyya, 2002), for resource allocation and to regulate supply and demand of the available resources. This economic-based framework offers an incentive to resource owners for contributing and sharing resources, and motivates resource users to think about trade-offs between the processing time (e.g., deadline) and computational cost (e.g., budget), depending on their QoS requirements. It is believed that this approach is essential for promoting the Grids as a mainstream computing paradigm, which could lead to the emergence of new service-oriented computing industry.

3. Clearinghouse Service Framework Introduction

To use GRID resources, there are several steps needed to complete these tasks. First of all, for a user to access the GRID, there must be a way where the user can identify what's available, and how various services are created. Thus information directory service, e.g. UDDI, is needed to locate resources, data banks, market registry for resource pricing. Metadata for resource capabilities is also needed. Second, user must be able to interact with & submit jobs to the Grid, which requires low-level service API's, authentication and trust mechanisms, and mechanisms for parallel processing. Finally, user must know how and where to obtain computed data, which needs secure file transfer protocols, file directory catalogs, enabling efficient retrieval and storage of data.

There are available tools and software to help Grid system designers in their tasks. For example, the Globus toolkit provides a peer-to-peer architecture for users to access remote resource using a set of APIs. The toolkit also provides a bag of service for resource discovery (Monitoring & Directory Service), secure resource access (Grid Security Infrastructure) and data transfer (GridFTP). Due to its widely deployment and way of distribution (opensource), The Globus has emerged to become a *de-facto* standard for Grid computing. Another competing standard comes from co-called Web Services that is initiated and leading by UN/CEFECT and OASIS, for e-Business uses.

As illustrated above, Grid Clearinghouse service is foreseeable to fulfill the market demand. A Clearinghouse can be identified as a middleware for integrating mandatory Grid services. A Clearinghouse provides central access for user authentication, enable dynamic resource sharing policies, and maintain accounts of participating enterprises/organizations. The clearinghouse will make the final decision of how to create resource suppliers and debit resource consumers. Finally, Clearinghouse should provide Grid market for resource trading. We can assume the clearinghouse is a regulating body of how suppliers would charge for their resources.

The basic functions of the Clearinghouse consist of:

(1) Job submission and management

(2) Resource trading between enterprises

(3) Resource usage monitoring (Grimshaw and W. Wulf, 1997).

The projected GRID Clearinghouse service framework is illustrated in Figure 1.

GRID Clearinghouse Service Framework

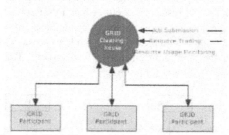

Figure 1 Grid Clearinghouse Service Framework

Clearinghouse service flow can be structured as the following steps:

Creation of the Application Service Agent (ASA)

Application service agent can be seen as a process that is dynamically created by the clearinghouse service host. The clearinghouse delegates the responsibility of user request management to the application service agent. The service agent acts on behalf of the user to find and acquire suitable resources to schedule jobs submitted by the user. The service agent also tracks the status of jobs submitted by the user, and negotiates with services providers, the price for resource consumption.

Submission of Job Application

The clearinghouse identifies the specification of the nature of the job. Locating or uploading of actual binaries to run the application. Feeding input data to server process and indicating paths or URL for output data then, exceed.

Application Service Agent accesses the Clearinghouse for the following information when submitting a job

When submitting a job, application service agent need to know the location of resource & capabilities, paths to application services on remote sites, URLs to obtain input data and output data. Resource consumption price proposed by enterprises is needed.

4. *Economic Considerations*

The Grid Clearinghouse service framework can be seen as a trading model from business perspective. From economic considerations, cost issue can be the major concern for resource consumers and suppliers.

The Clearinghouse organizes enterprises as consortium for sharing resources and enforces sharing by resource trading. Resource trading is about how enterprises go about exchanging their computing resources with each other. To trade resources in the Clearinghouse, users of the clearinghouse must belong to exactly one domain or enterprise. Exchange of resources occurs when a user consumes resources from another enterprise. When this happens, the clearinghouse will compute the cost of consumption so that debit and credits can be made to the accounts of the consuming enterprise and the supplying enterprise respectively. The Clearinghouse resource trading model is shown in Figure 2.

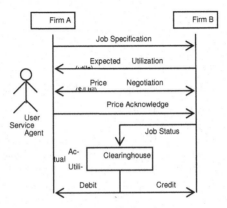

Figure 2 Resource Sharing Model (Percival Xavier, 2003)

For resource trading to occur, the following must exist; Resource contribution must first be quantified. Quantification of resource usage is termed utilization. A pricing strategy for enterprises is able to sell their resource as profitable as possible yet maximizing utilization. Accounting mechanisms must be implemented to charge users for using remote resources registered to the clearinghouse.

Resource pricing are negotiations performed between consumers and suppliers There are generally 3 modes of interactions for resource pricing, viz. one consumer - many suppliers, many consumers- one supplier, many consumers - many suppliers.

In the case of one consumer - many suppliers: suppliers compete to lower their prices until it is no longer feasible. Once price equilibrium is established the consumer will select a supplier and acknowledge the price established. For the case of many consumers, one supplier: Consumers must bid a price as high as possible to acquire a resource. Once the auction ceases, the consumer that provides the highest bid will obtain the resource. For the last scenario of many consumers, many supplier; Consumers may form alliances for resource consumption so that they can share the total cost of acquiring similar resource.

5. Grid Economic Service Architecture Introduction

The concepts and procedures we formulate as above need operational mechanism to realize in certain details, e.g. make the services chargeable. Economic Service Architecture (ESA) Architecture initiated by OGSA serves a reference model.

The architecture of the Grid Economic Services Architecture infrastructure is illustrated in figure 3, showing how the grid service that is to be sold as a Chargeable Grid Service (CGS) interacts with the Grid Payment System (GPS) and the resource usage services. (Daniel Minoli, 2005)

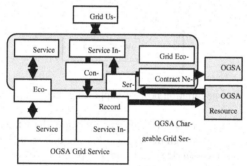

Figure3: Computational grid service being sold as a Chargeable Grid Service (Daniel Minoli, 2005)

Discussions identified one key requirement, e.e, that the underlying Grid service interface has not to be changed, but only be extended, by the wrapping of a grid service as a CGS. This would allow existing clients to interact with a CGS even if the client interface had been generated for the underlying GRID service.

This basic architecture exploits the transient nature of a grid service to encapsulate the cost of using the service within its Service Data Elements (SDE). All changes in state of the grid service (from the initial advertisement, establishing the cost of its use, to the acceptance of this cost, through to its eventual use) are encapsulated through the creation of new services.

Job Submission and Scheduling

According to the typical user workflow of computing, user interact Grid from UI to submit job, match make the best resources, check job status, and retrieve job results. Job match-making and distributing is in charged by the resource broker (RB) and the workload manager. The problem is that there is no standard way to submit job, this work is fully depend on the job scheduling system deployed. Resource brokering and job dispatching mechanism are also different by systems.

Our focus is based on the generic portal of economic/chargeable Grid applications, by employing a job wrapper for common job descriptions and virtual queuing system for the dynamic job execution management. The whole management should still base on workload management, resource broker and charging services such as contract negotiation. We have developed the mechanism (Figure 4) as a decision tool by price negotiation and integrated the Clearinghouse applications as described in section 3 into the Grid service system. Hereby, the price negotiation becomes a function of costs, workload and time, where the fuzzy functions can be employed when a rapid decision is needed.

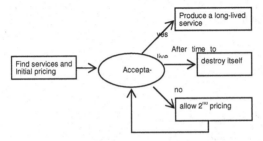

Figure 4 The price negotiation process supporting service sharing

The process shown in Figure 4 illustrates the negotiation how the user finds a service and requests a price through the Request-Pricing operation. The pricing is encapsulated in a short-lived service that is not acceptable to the user and the chosen economic model supports a second call to the Request-Pricing operation to produce a section short-lived service. The user has only two choices: to reject the price and let the service destroy itself after given time or to accept the pricing, which produces a long-lived service specifically created for the user. The pricing of this service may have two stages, a single stage or many stages. The detailed protocols need to support this form of interaction can be described as Figure 5.

The Chargeable Grid Service (CGS)

The CGS represents the abstraction of a grid service that has been enabled to support economic interaction. SDE includes pricing, usage, price liability and testimonial.

Figure 5 Price-negotiation-centric Chargeable Grid Service

The SDEs provided by the CGS are in addition to those defined within the OGSI Specification. These contain static and dynamic metadata relating to the economic use of the service. This list of SDE is not exhaustive and should be expanded and adapted as the requirements from the economic models develop. For example, instead of using real currency within the refund or compensation SDE, a service may choose to give credit. This could be represented as a currency exchangeable only with the services run by a specific service provider. The SDE constitute a service –specific advertising element and some of these SDEs may only be relevant at different stages of the CGS lifetime.

Service Interface Definition: It is proposed that the Grid Economic Service Interface (GESI) should support a number of operations to facilitate the GESA. The first of these is a *factory operation* to allow the creation of new instances of this particular CGS. It is envisaged that many of these CGSs will have a multistage process to define the final cost of the service to the user, for example, negotiation, auctioning, and so on. To enable each mode of interaction, the initial act of any CGS on being contacted by a user will be to create a new service instance to deal with the requested interaction method.

The Grid Payment System

The GPS provides a service to a payment infrastructure that is itself defined outside the GESA document. The purpose of this section is to define the interaction between the GPS and other entities within the GESA. No implementation details are specified within the GESA. However, the GPS could be implemented by any infrastructure with an account-based abstraction. This could include systems based around electronic cash, credit cards, accountancy packages with periodic reconciliation, prepaid accounts, service tokens, and so on. The "currency" sued in these transactions need not be recognized or supported by a large community. A currency could relate to service tokens allocated within a specific service centre or virtual organization. If the CGS is willing to accept more than one currency to pay for service usage, then this may be specified within its economic SDEs.

SDE hereby includes Currency, Banker Payment/Method, TrustedUser, PrivilegedUser (3P service)

Interface definition: The GPS supports the following operations. As the current authorization model for GridServices has yet to be defined, one uses the following classification for these operations:

1 Unprivileged : A normal GSI authenticated client connection is sufficient.

2 Trusted : A GSI authenticated client whose DN is registered as an account holder in the GPS or is contained in the TrustedUser SDE.

3 Privileged : A GSI authenticated client whose DN is contained in the PrivilegedUser SDE

GPSHold Service

This service instance encapsulates the duration and amount of money being held on behalf of the client. OGSI standard lifetime management tools can be used to extend the length of service. The hold on the currency ends when this service instance expires or is terminated by the client. The service can only be terminated by the declared owner—the entity requesting the hold.

SDE : The current OGSI specification does not deal with any form of access control within SDEs.

Interface Definition : This service's primary function is to encapsulate the "reservation" of money from a specified account. The amount encapsulated by the reservation is immutable. Therefore, the only operations =that may be performed on the service instance are effectively related to the lifetime management of the reservation, and this may be restricted by the GPS during service creation.

The Grid CurrencyExchange Service

The Grid CurrencyExchange Service provides a service to a currency exchange infrastructure that is itself defined outside this document. The purpose within this section is to define the interaction between the GCES and other entities within the GESA. The GCES could be implemented b any infrastructure with a currency-based abstraction. This could include systems based around electronic cash, credit cards, service tokens, and so on.

The "currency" used in these transactions need not be recognized or supported by a large community. A currency could relate to service tokens allocated within a specific service centre or virtual organization.

1 Service Data Elements : exchangeRate, Exchange Commission

6. Results and Summary

A rational pricing and billing mechanism for realizing GRID in business environment has been addressed. This paper explores the potential clearinghouse-like service for Grid Computing. We have decomposed Grid system architecture, identified potential design issues in IT service environment. The result is to transform an abstract utility concept into concrete service collaboration.

The resources that are coupled in Grid computing environment are distributed and different individuals or organizations own each one of them and they have their own access policy, cost and mechanism. The resource owners manage and control resources using their favorite resource management and scheduling system and the Grid users are expected to honor that make sure they do not interfere with resource owners' policies. They may charge different prices for different Grid users for their resource usage and it may vary from time to time.

The economic-based Grid Clearinghouse service framework is proposed in this paper. When the user submits an application for execution, they expect that the application be executed within a given deadline and cost. There is no single perfect solution that meets all user requirements; hence this promotes the need for tailored Grid schedulers for each class of applications.

The concepts brought by CleaningHouse can be realized by means trading and billing services after ESA. This paper points out the mechanisms necessary for the economic services, viz. ChargeableService, GridPaymentSystem and GPSHold-Service. The CurrencyExchange is important for international business services. The effects of perceived issues and potential Clearinghouse services are worthy of further investigation.

As a whole, the outcome of this paper includes:
1 A Cleaninghouse-like Framework for Economic GRID Services
2 A method for managing the resource trading behavior and economic services needed for GRID and SOA platforms
3 Useful Software packages (interfaces) to facilitate the economic services, including billing and payment.
4 Solutions for GRID/Web Service Providers to do resource trading and to integrate them into a uniform computing environment.

References

[1]. A Vahdat. Toward Wide-Area Resource Allocation. In Proceedings of the International Conference Parallel and Distributed Processing Techniques and Applications (PDPTA'99). Page 930-936. June (1999)

[2]. Daniel Minoli, "A Networking Approach to Grid Computing", WILEY, (2005)

[3]. D. Minoli: "An networking approach to GRID Computing", Wiley, (2005).

[4]. Eric Newcomer, Greg Lomow, Understanding SOA with Web Services, Addison Wesley, (2005).

[5]. G. Banga, P. Drushnel, and J. C. Mogul. Resource Containers: A New Facility for Resource Management in Server Systems. In Proceeding of the 3rd USENIX Symposium on Operating Systems Design and Implementation (OSDI'99). Pp45-58, January (1999).

[6]. Grimshaw and W. Wulf, The Legion Vision of Worldwide Virtual Computer, Communications of the ACM, vol. 40(1), January (1997)

[7]. IBM Grid Computing, "What is grid computing", http://www-1.ibm.com/grid/about_grid/what_is.shtml, accessed 12 Jan (2004)

152

[8]. Johannes K. Chiang: "Developing a Governmental Long-term Archive Management System on Semantic Grid", 2005 PNC Annual Conference and Joint Meetings, Oct. (2005), Hawaii USA.

[9]. Johannes K. Chiang et al: "Investigation of for the architecture and technological procedures for long-term preservation of digital archives. Research Report, National Archive and Records Bureau, ROC, Taipei, 15 Dec. (2004).

[10]. Klaus Wehrle, Frank Pahlke, Hartmut Ritter, and Daniel Muller ,"The Linux Networking Architecture", Pearson Prentice Hall, (2005).

[11]. Lazar and N. Semret, "Auctions for Network Resource Sharing", TR 468-97-02, Columbia University, Feb (1997)

[12]. M. Aron, P. Drushnel, and W. Zwaenepoel. "Cluster Reserves: A Mechanism for Resource Management in Cluster-based Network Servers". In Proceedings of the International Conference on Measurement and Modeling of Computer Systems (SIGMETRICS2000). Page 90-101. June (2000).

[13]. M. D. Stefano, "Distributed Data Management for Grid Computing", Wiley, (2005).

[14]. M. Li and M. Baker: "The Grid core technologies", Wiley, (2005).

[15]. Oram, "Peer-to-Peer: Harnessing the Power of Disruptive Technologies", O'Reilly Press, USA, (2001)

[16]. Percival Xavier, "A Clearinghouse for Resource Management in Campus Grid", NanYang Technological University, 4 March, (2003)

[17]. Rajkumar Buyya, "Economic based Distributed Resource Management Scheduling for Grid Computing", Monash University, 12 April, (2002)

[18]. R. Moore, "Using Data Grids to Manage Distributed Data", Lecture slides for PNC 2004 Annual Conference, Taipei, Taiwan, 17-22 October, (2004).

ABOUT THE AUTHORS

Prof. Johannes K. Chiang works now at the Department of MIS of National Chengchi University Taipei and as the Chairman of the ITMA on Taiwan. He received the academic degree of Doctor in Engineering Science (*Dr.-Ing., Summa Cum laude*) from the University (RWTH) of Aachen, Germany. His current research interests include "Data and Semantic GRID", "Business Intelligence and Data Mining", e-Business and ebXML, Business Data Communication. Besides, he serves as a consultant for government agencies in Taiwan, and an active member of various domestic as well as international affiliations, such as ICANN, UN/CEFACT and TWNIC. Before 1995, he has been a research fellow at RWTH Aachen and Manager for EU/CEC projects.

Kiekang is a PhD student at National Cheng Chi University. He participate various IT communities. He is the board member of IMA (Information Management Association) in Taiwan, and IT director of DHL Express Taiwan.

Part III   Grid Middleware & Interoperability

Interoperability between gLite and GOS

Yongjian Wang, Yaodong Cheng, Gang Chen

Institute of High Energy Physics, Chinese Academy of Sciences, Beijing, China

Abstract

Interoperability among different grid middlewares with different architectures is not a trivial task, i.e. gLite, used in European grid infrastructure EGEE, and GOS, used in the Chinese grid infrastructure CNGRID infrastructure. But it's necessary in order to extend the European GRID infrastructure for e-Science to China and vice verse. The aim of our work is to facilitate scientific data transfer and processing in a first sample of scientific communities that have already strong collaborations between Europe and China. The interoperability between gLite and GOS middlewares and, then, the interconnection between EGEE and CNGRID infrastructures, is fundamental to achieve this goal.

This paper presents the interoperability solution adopted during our work, including job submission, data transfer, and information services. The prototype implementation of a gateway for achieving interoperability is discussed and preliminary results are also presented.

1   Introduction

The term interoperability refers to the capability of different programs to work together by understanding and executing commands from one another, exchanging data via a common set of business procedures, and reading/writing files using the same protocols.

Grid middlewares [1, 2, and 3] may have very different software architectures and adopt different protocols. For this reason, achieving full interoperability between two different grid middlewares is not an easy task. Job submission and control, output retrieval, data management, etc. should be taken into account and properly managed by the other middleware involved.

Several existing joint research activities, between Europe and China involve analysis of large volume of data and require large amounts of computing power. The main objective of our work is to facilitate exchange and processing of scientific data using both the EGEE and CNGRID infrastructures. Moreover, the inter-

S.C. Lin and E. Yen (eds.), *Production Grids in Asia: Applications, Developments and Global Ties*, DOI 10.1007/978-1-4419-0046-3_13,
© Springer Science + Business Media, LLC 2010

operability of the European and Chinese grid infrastructures provides the research and education communities of the two regions with transparent access to a larger world widely distributed amount of storage and computing resources allowing the development of a new scale of powerful applications.

This paper presents our work which is performed to achieve interoperability between gLite [9], the grid middleware of the EGEE [7] infrastructure, and GOS [16], the grid middleware of the CNGRID [15] infrastructure. Our work aims to harmonize, for the benefit of several e-Science applications, the European and Chinese e-Infrastructures in terms of computing resources, services, and application software.

The paper is organized as follows. Section 2 describes the EGEE infrastructure and the gLite middleware and the CNGRID infrastructure and the GOS middleware. Section 3 introduces some basic concepts about grid middlewares interoperability. Section 4 explains our solution to make gLite and GOS interoperable. Section 5, the testbed created to test our solution is described and some preliminary results are also presented. Finally, in section 6, we reach conclusions and point out our future work.

2 EGEE and CNGrid Overview

The Enabling Grids for E-sciencE (EGEE) [7] project draws together over 1,000 scientists and engineers from more than 90 institutions in 32 countries worldwide, offering them an advanced Grid Infrastructure available around the clock. EGEE is used by applications from many scientific disciplines, as high energy physics, life sciences, geology, computational chemistry and so on. It is a general purpose infrastructure that will be used by any scientific research especially where the time and resources needed for running the applications are considered impractical with traditional IT infrastructures.

The EGEE grid is composed by over 36,000 CPU available to users 24 hours a day, 7 days a week, in addition to 5 Petabytes (5 million of Gigabytes) storage, and 30,000 concurrent jobs run on the average. gLite [9] is the middleware used for grid computing in EGEE. It was developed as part of the EGEE Project and it is the result of the collaborative efforts of more than 80 people in 12 different academic and industrial research centres. gLite provides a set of services that allow users to make use of the huge resources of the EGEE infrastructure in an easy way, hiding the complexity of the infrastructure. gLite services comprise security, monitoring, job and data management and were developed to follow a service-oriented architecture.

China National Grid (CNGrid for short hereafter) was developed under the support of China's National High-tech R&D Program (the so called 863 Program). CNGrid [15] consists of ten nodes across the country, including two major nodes, Computer Network & Information Centre of CAS (CNIC, CAS) in Beijing and the Shanghai Supercomputer Centre (SSC, Shanghai) in Shanghai, and eight ordinary nodes. Equipped with the high performance computers and grid software developed in China, CNGrid forms an open grid environment for supporting applications in the fields of research, resource and environment, service and manufacture. The aggregated computing capacity of CNGrid exceeds 25 TFlops. The total storage capacity is over 300TB.

The grid software, CNGrid GOS [16], enables the operation of CNGrid and grid applications by supporting resource sharing and cooperative works, which makes CNGrid a testbed for scientific research, technology development, and application demonstration. The latest release is CNGrid GOS v3.1, which is available since October 2008. GOSv3.1 optimizes the previous versions with enhanced functionalities. And now more than 50 grid applications are deployed in CNGrid, and there are also some eleven national-wide applications deployed in the CNGrid environment, including Scientific Data Grid (SDG), Bioinformation Application Grid (BAGrid), etc. But during our work, we mainly based on the GOSv2.1 and we will migrate our work to support the GOSv3.1.

3   Grid Middlewares Interoperability

The Interoperability among grid middlewares with different architectures is not a trivial task. Generally speaking, the level of interoperability strongly depends on how closely the infrastructures have to work together. The first level of interoperability, which is the basic requirement, is to supply users with the possibility of submitting their jobs from one infrastructure to the other and vice-versa. The second level is reached by providing the capability of controlling the submitted jobs from the initiator. Then the problem of data interoperability has to be addressed. The final level of interoperability is achieved by implementing interoperable services so that the user does not need to care about the middleware, but just access the services from whatever available portal, in a transparent and ubiquitous way.
There are several solutions to implement interoperability among different grid infrastructures, including user driven approach, gateway approach and standardization of grid interfaces.

3.1   User Driven Approach

In this approach, user deploys multiple client toolkits of different grid infrastructures, then applies different grid credentials to submit job to the target grid. If target applications are deployed in the target grids, it is easy to run jobs.

This approach is simply, but it is not transparent and needs more work for end user. Atlas adopts this method and implements its workload management system PanDA [23], which is pilot-based and can use any job submission service (CondorG, local batch, EGEE, Condor glide-ins ...) to deliver jobs.

3.2   The Gateway Approach

A gateway is a bridge between different grid infrastructures which supplies end users with the possibility of submitting and controlling the whole lifecycle of their jobs from one infrastructure to the other and vice-versa. Through this approach, the user does not need to care about the middleware differences, but just access the services from whatever available portal, in a transparent and ubiquitous way. The gateway plays very import roles in this method. A gateway installation belongs to multiple grid infrastructures simultaneously. So jobs from Grid A can be scheduled into the gateway, and then are transformed and submitted to Grid B. It is also the same for jobs from Grid B.

This approach are widely adopted by many bilateral interoperability projects, such as LCG and ARC[24], gLite and Naregi[25], gLite and ENEA-Grid[26], ENEA-Grid and Unicore, GOS and gLite[27] etc. However, a gateway is a single point of failure because all loads are passing through it. If gateway breaks, the integrated grid will disappear. It is necessary to deploy multiple gateways to improve the availability, for example a special data gateway is needed in data-intensive HEP applications.

3.3   Standardization of Grid Interface

The goal of Grid is to integrate the worldwide heterogeneous computing resources, storage resources to form a virtual supercomputer. However, current grid middlewares and infrastructures were developed independently. It is difficult to achieve the goal for the moment. Bilateral grid interoperability is not general method, and is also a time-consuming work. If all of the grid systems are to follow standard interfaces, user can submit jobs and transfer data transparently.

Open Grid Forum has set up a special working group GIN-CG (Grid Interoperation Now Community Group) [28] to identify islands of interoperability. Currently, major grid projects in the world join the group, including EGEE, NAREGI, UK National Grid, NorduGrid, OSG, PRAGMA, TeraGrid and so on. GIN-CG focuses on security, job management, data management, information systems, and grid operations. However, there is still a long way to achieve mature grid interoperability standards.

4. gLite-GOS Interoperability

gLite and GOS middlewares adopt very different architectures and for this reason the "gateway" approach to make them interoperable seemed to be the best practicable approach. The role of the gateway is to translate requests coming from one middleware into requests compatible with the other. Requests such as job submission, job-control, output retrieval, and data management have to be taken into account.

It should be pointed out that a method for sharing the "knowledge" between the two middlewares about the status of resources available in their respective infrastructure is the basis for a trivial interoperation prototyping.

4.1 Primary Design Principles

Interoperability gateway in charges of transparently job forwarding and data transfer among different grid infrastructures, and it's easy to become a performance bottleneck.

The primary design principles of our interoperability gateway are modularity and high throughput.

> Modularity is the first design principle, because we want to follow a generic approach for interoperability as it usually consists of several independent blocks such as data staging, script parsing, authentication and authorization, and so on.

> High throughput is the second principle because the gateway lies between CNGrid and EGEE so thousands of jobs may go through it every day.

IoC [17] (Inversion of Control) is adopted as the way to instantiate and manage the lifecycles of different atomic modules. The SEDA [18] (Staged Event Driven Architecture) model was also adopted to assemble different atomic modules into pipelines for different purposes.

Figure 1 shows the conceptual architecture of our interoperability gateway. It basically consists of three different components: thread pool, scheduler and the pipeline. The pipeline is assembled in the runtime. A fixed number of threads are allocated in advance and maintained in the thread pool which will be used by the scheduler to drive the processing logics encapsulated in the pipeline.

Moreover, the processing logics encapsulated in the pipeline and executed by the thread pool in the runtime is stateless. It means that different instances of the gateway can be configured to connect to the infrastructure running GOS and gLite. In this way, the gateway approach also guarantees the scalability of the system.

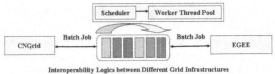

Fig. 1 the Conceptual Architecture of Gateway

4.2   Job Management Services

The Job Service is one of the main functional modules of grid middlewares and provides a user-friendly way for using the underlying computing resources. In order to allow the CNGrid users to use computing and storage resources of EGEE, and vice-versa, the gateway must have the capability to forward batch jobs received from one grid infrastructure to the other. The forwarding should be transparent the end user.

The Job Service has relationships with many other modules such as the data management module, the resource information discovery & selection module, the authentication and authorization module and so on. So, implementing the job management services in the gateway seems to be a relatively complex task.
In this section, we will focus on the following two issues:

➢   Necessary conversion in the gateway;
➢   Extension of functionalities of the CNGrid GOS Job Manager and the EGEE LCG CE for transparently   forwarding of jobs between the EGEE and CNGrid;

4.2.1   Necessary conversion in the gateway

Different batch job process mechanisms are adopted by different grid middlewares. There are two core functional components in the batch job processing: job description language, and the way to submit jobs. Although OGSA-BES [19] has defined a standard job submission interface and the JSDL [13] is chosen as the standard job description language, proprietary interfaces are widely deployed and work well and it is difficult and impractical to replace them immediately. Figure 2 depicts the role of the gateway in the job management service.

The pipeline is built using the conceptual architecture introduced in section 4.1. It consists of different stages so that different modules such as data management, security, resource scheduling, etc. can be easily integrated into the batch job process.

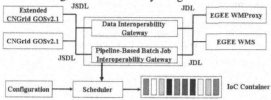

Fig. 2 the Job Management Service Process

Because of the differences between job management mechanisms, two issues must be handled during cross-domain job management:

➤ Job Description Language;
➤ Job Submission Manner.

Job description language is used to define job requirements, its major elements includes: command definition, resource requirement definition and data staging definition. Different syntax is used to describe job requirements in different job description languages, a conversion must be performed between the job descriptor languages that adopted by CNGrid GOS and EGEE gLite.

Table 1. Difference in Job Service

Middleware	Job Descriptor Language	Job Submission Manner
CNGrid GOS	JSDL	Portal, Web Service
EGEE gLite	JDL	Command Line, Web Service

Table 1 compares the job submission mechanisms in CNGrid GOS and EGEE gLite. Different job description languages are adopted but both of them support Web Service-based job submission manner. The gateway needs to develop a converter for syntax conversion between JSDL and JDL (Job Description Language) [20] while the common web service interface can be used to submit jobs.

The job description language is used to define necessary information for batch job processing, and the major elements including: command definition, resource requirement definition and data staging definition. JSDL and JDL adopt different syntaxes to carry on job information, and a conversion must be done between JSDL and JDL during job processing by gateway.

Table . 2 Mapping between JSDL and JDL

Job Descriptor Language	GOS JSDL	gLite JDL
Application	JobDefinition/Application/ POSIXApplication/Executable	Executable
Argument	JobDefinition/Application/ POSIXApplication/Arguments	Arguments
Data Transfer	JobDefinition/DataStaging	InputSandbox/ OutputSSandBox

Table 2 maps the major elements between JSDL and JDL. It is just a syntax-level mapping; the semantic-level mapping is discussed in the rest of this paper.

4.2.2   Extensions to GOS and gLite

The difficulties of forwarding jobs lie in how the interoperability gateway can receive jobs submitted by users without any perturbation of the original resource scheduling mechanism used by CNGrid GOS and EGEE gLite. It is a relative complex problem mainly because scheduler mechanisms such as Meta Scheduler in CNGrid GOS and gLite WMS/LCG RB in EGEE are different and there is no standard interface now.

We solved this problem by extending CNGrid GOS Job Manager and EGEE LCG CE. The extended CNGrid GOS Job Manager and the gLite/LCG CE will forward the received batch job to the other grid infrastructure through the interoperability gateway instead of processing it locally. Using this approach, the CNGrid end users can submit their batch jobs using the GOS supported mechanism and the batch jobs will be transparently forwarded to EGEE. Of course, the system works in the other direction as well.

Fig. 3 Extended GOS JobManager

Figure 3 shows the extended GOS batch service which consists of five different components:

➢ Job Manager: an extensible plug-in framework which can instantiate different RMS (Resource Management System) according to the configuration;

➢ OpenPBS/LSF-based RMS System: supporting interaction to OpenPBS and LSF;

➢ gLite-based RMS System: supporting interaction with gLite WMProxy;

➢ WS-Interface: a Web Service that exposes the functionalities of Job Manager;

➢ WS-Client: a Web Service client used to interact with WS-Interface for batch job submission, job status monitoring, and so on;

We added a gLite-based Resource Management System (RMS) System which can interact with the WMProxy module in gLite for job submission and monitoring. This RMS will forward batch jobs from the CNGrid GOS users to the EGEE gLite resources for execution.

We choose to extend the functionalities of LCG-CE, which is widely deployed in EGEE environment, in order to transparently forward batch jobs from EGEE to CNGrid. Figure 4 shows how the LCG-CE is enhanced.

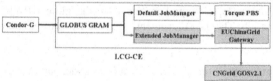

Fig. 4 Extended LCG-CE JobManager

EGEE end users interact to the Resource Broker (i.e., the LCG RB or the gLite WMS) through the command-line or the Web Service interface. The Resource Broker first contacts the Information Service and selects a CE to execute the batch job. Then, it submits the batch job to the LCG-CE using Condor-G. When the LCG-CE receives the batch job from the Resource Broker, the GRAM component (GRAM LCG CE) will instantiate a corresponding Job Manager according to the configuration. We provide a special JobManager for CNGrid (Extended Job Manager for CNGrid) which will forward the entire received batch job to CNGrid for execution.

4.3   Data Management System

Data transfer between different grid infrastructures is the basis of job interoperability. The goal of data interoperability is to enable users of one infrastructure to use the storage resources and access files in the other infrastructure and vice-versa.

In order to implement effectively data interoperability, we should identify differences between the two middlewares in data processing. The major differences are in the following aspects:

➢ Storage of data: in gLite, small amount of data for a job can be stored using the temporary storage of Resource Broker (RB); while large volume data should be firstly stored in the Storage Element (SE) by end user and downloaded by the Work Node (WN) when the job is running. However, GOS does not distinguish small or large volume of data; it just stores all data on the FTP server.

➢ Transfer Protocol: GridFTP/GSIFTP protocol [6] is widely used for data transfer in gLite, while in the GOS universe the simple FTP protocol is used.

4.3.1 Small Scale Data Transfer

In gLite, small data can be associated directly to a job. Data are described/ contained by/in the InputSandbox and the OutputSandbox parameters of the job specified in the JDL files, and usual data volumes are less than 20MB. gLite transfers the data specified in Input/OutputSandbox from the gLite UI/WN to the gLite WN/UI with the job. The data movements are performed using the GridFTP protocol.

When a job is submitted from a gLite UI to a GOS node, our interoperability solution ensures that the gLite Input/OutputSandbox data is properly managed. This result is achieved thanks to the conversion between JDL and JSDL on the gateway, which plays again as a forwarding node. Also, the transfer protocol will be changed from GridFTP to FTP. The process is depicted in Figure 5 which shows the operation of the gateway when a jobs passes through it.

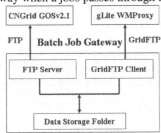

Fig. 5 Forward Based Small data transfer

There is no specially data interoperability gateway for small scale data transfer. The batch job gateway supports both FTP and GridFTP, it in charges of interacting with GOS and gLite.

4.3.2 Large Scale Data Transfer

In this section we will devote our attention to large data volumes interoperability. Hybrid solutions for data movement do have strong impact on performances, especially when an intermediate element such as a gateway is used. The solution of focusing on a point-to-point data transfer seems to be feasible. The Usage of managed resources and their APIs (SRM, SRB) should help.

As a general solution, interfaces compliant with the Storage Resource Manager [5] (SRM) for data management is introduced. This interface acts as a higher level bridge above the low level transfer protocols in order to setup an effective and transparent data exchange service. All the end users can use a series of uniform commands provided by the SRM client to access the storage resources.

We have extended the *BeStMan* which is a full implementation of *SRM* v2.2, developed by Lawrence Berkeley National Laboratory. In our extension, we add multiple transfer protocol support, including FTP, HTTPs. It means you can access the same data using different protocol which depends on your need as Figure 6 depicts.

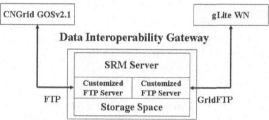

Fig. 6 SRM-based Point-to-Point Data Transfer

GOS provides good support for FTP. We add many features based on basic functionalities that support by the underlying protocol, including cache, asynchronous data transfer, failure recovery(restart from last failure) etc. Our extended SRM server provides a well support for FTP protocol and can support standard FTP client. It means that all the data that stores to SRM server using GridFTP protocol by EGEE end users can be access directly by CNGrid User. The username token is used for authentication here.

GridFTP is the most widely used transfer protocol in EGEE environment which is not supported in CNGrid environment. Our extended SRM server can support the standard GridFTP protocol and the EGEE end user can just use the familiar globus-url-copy command to upload/download data to/from it.

4.4   Authentication and Authorization

Due to the need of developing a higher level of trust between users and owners of the resources belonging to the two different grid infrastructures, the cross-domain security issue seems to be one of the most relevant challenges in the design of the gateway.

The gateway has to provide the authentication and authorization functionalities. To reach this goal, we have defined two different security modules in the gateway. The first module is the Identity Mapping Service and the second module is the Security Token Service.

The Identity Mapping Service is used to map identities between heterogeneous identity management infrastructures, such as EGEE and CNGrid. Figure 7 depicts the role of the Identity Mapping Service when a GOS user invokes a service deployed in the EGEE/GILDA [10] environment.

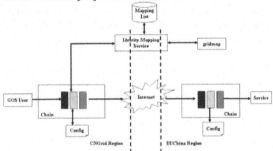

Fig. 7 the Identity Mapping Service

The Security Token Service is used to centrally store security tokens in order to allow users from different domains to retrieve the corresponding tokens when necessary, as defined in the OGSA-BES (OGSA Basic Execution Services) specification [19]. We have developed a prototype of the Security Token Service which is compliant with the WS-Trust Specification [21]. Figure 8 shows the conceptual architecture of the Security Token Service.

There are some functional overlaps between the Identity Mapping Service and the Security Token Service. The Identity Mapping Service is used in the currently implemented version of the gateway.

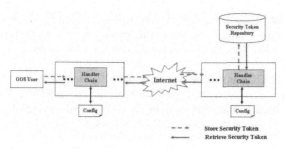

Fig. 8 the Security Token Service

4.5 Information and Monitoring Services

Each grid middleware has its own information service which collects information from the resources such as available CPUs, available memory, etc. and monitors the status of submitted jobs. The process of discovering resources and their states is fundamental to reach a real interoperability between CNGrid GOS and EGEE gLite because an effective resource selection mechanism relies on a good knowledge of the current status of the resources. We believe the key point for implementing interoperability is how to publish resources' information which comes from individual grid communities.

The BDII (Berkeley Database Information Index) [11] service developed by the LCG project, and adopted in gLite, is a flexible and effective information service. Given that the BDII is adopted by the gLite middleware, what we have to take care of is to publish resources' information from GOS to gLite to achieve information service interoperability.

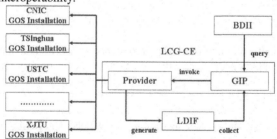

Fig. 9 publishing information from GOS to gLite

Figure 9 shows the process of publishing resource information from GOS to gLite. The BDII sends a request for querying resources' information to some LCG-CE nodes which act as the gateway in our design. By developing a customer-defined provider procedure which interfaces with GIP (Generic Information provider)

[12], the gateway connects to remote GOS nodes using the SSH protocol, and extracts resource information compliant with the GLUE schema from the local resource such as CPU load, memory usage, batch system status, etc.

We delegate all GOS nodes belonging to the GOS domain as a LCG-CE node while using the gateway-method proposed here. So, on the EGEE side, users are just required to query information from the GOS domain in the usual way, and query gLite information through the BDII on GOS side.

5. gLite-GOS Interoperability Testbed

Figure 10 depicts the test environment. Our testbed consists of machines from IHEP, CAS China and INFN, Italy. Both CNGrid user and EGEE user can submit jobs using their familiar manners, and the jobs will be forwarded to other grid middlewares for execution.

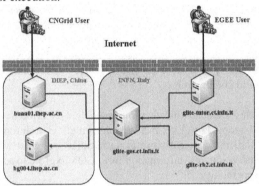

Fig. 10 Interoperability Test Environment

We have installed a first interoperability prototype in a full testbed to test our solutions. The testbed has been deployed on the Grid INFN Laboratory for Dissemination Activities (GILDA, https://gilda.ct.infn.it), the de-facto standard training infrastructure of EGEE.

This first prototype allows user to submit jobs which manage simple data from gLite to GOS and vice versa. Figure 11 shows the testbed we setup for the gLite-GOS interoperability. The testbed consists of three different parts:

➢ CNGrid GOS environment
  • portal.ct.infn.it is a full GOS portal installation. It uses extended JobManager that forwards received batch job to EGEE;
  • gos.ct.infn.it is a full GOS node and uses OpenPBS as local resource management system;

➤ EGEE GLite environment
- glite-rb2.ct.infn.it is a LCG-RB available on the GILDA infrastructure with the WMProxy module installed;
- glite-tutor.ct.infn.it is a glite User Interface (UI) available on GILDA From which the end user can submit batch jobs and monitor their status;

➤ Gateway used for interoperability
- glite-gos.ct.infn.it is the gateway between the two infrastructures which in charges of both job and data interoperability.

The testbed has run stably for more than one year, and it has been successfully used for a live demo performed during the final project review of EUChinaGrid project which is an EU-FP6 supported project, in Brussels, Belgium on April, 15th, 2008.

5.1   Performance Measurements

Performance measurements have been done considering two different aspects:

➤ Job Execution Time: provides a measure of the overhead introduced by the gateway;

➤ Throughput: the Gateway lies between CNGrid and EGEE, high throughput support is very important for production use;

The Gateway is installed on a machine with two Intel(R) Xeon(TM) CPU 2.40GHz CPU and all the tests described below have been done with this machine.

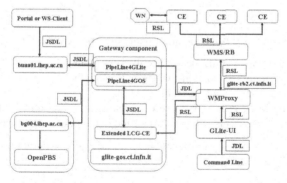

Fig. 11 gLite-GOS interoperability Testbed

Table 3 compares the Job Execution Time of a simple job (Linux command "host-name") submitted in a pure GOS environment with the execution time of the same job submitted from the gLite environment to a GOS resource through the Gateway.

Table . 3. gLite-GOS Measurement

Pure GOS	Through Gateway to GOS	GW overhead and Interoperability cost in %
92sec	143sec	35.7%
78sec	136sec	42.6%
95sec	143sec	33.6%
70sec	125sec	44.0%
100sec	147sec	32.0%
avg.	avg.	avg.
87sec	138sec	37.58%

Table 4 compares the Job Execution Time of a simple job (Linux command "hostname") submitted in a pure gLite environment with the execution time of the same job submitted from the GOS environment to a gLite resource through the gateway.

Table . 4. GOS-gLite Measurement

Pure gLite	Through Gateway to GLite	GW overhead and Interoperability cost in %
376sec	442sec	14.9%
432sec	490sec	11.8%
371sec	441sec	15.9%
353sec	410sec	13.9%
353sec	417sec	15.3%
avg.	avg.	avg.
377sec	440sec	14.36%

CNGrid GOS processes batch job faster than gLite for the following reasons:

➢ CNGrid GOS performs meta-scheduling on client side, when the job is successfully submitted so, it just needs to dispatch the job to the target computing resource saving a lot of time;

➢ The scheduling process is more complex in gLite. Moreover, the delay in job status renew causes difficulties to find out the exact job execution time;

Table 5 shows the gateway resources status and the job execution time with different throughputs.

Table. 5. Throughput and Average Execution Time

Throughput N. Jobs (GOS-gLite, gLite-GOS)	CPU [%]	Mem. [%]	GOS-gLite Resp. Time (avg.) [sec]	gLite-GOS Resp. Time (avg.) [sec]
5 (5;0)	25.4	13.8	429	×

5 (2;3)	45.7	13.7	458	127
5 (0;5)	52.8	13.2	×	142
10 (10;0)	33.2	13.5	449	×
10 (5;5)	65.2	13.8	457	151
10 (0;10)	83.4	13.4	×	204
15 (0;15)	85.9	13.3	×	211
20 (0;20)	92.1	13.2	×	232

Table 5 shows an average usage of CPU and Memory. There is not a large data transfer, so increasing the number of concurrent jobs has little influence on memory usage. Increasing the number of GOS-gLite jobs number has also a little influence on CPU usage. A New JVM is launched when a new job is received from the gLite environment so increasing the number of gLite-GOS jobs has, on the contrary, strong influence on CPU usage.

6. Conclusions and outlook

Interconnecting the most relevant grid infrastructures in Europe and China, EGEE and CNGRID, is very important for many scientific applications which allow researchers of the two regions, Europe and China, to access computing and data resources which were not available before This will certainly change the way of doing scientific research.

The gateway-based interoperability approach proposed in this paper works well and seems to be a valid solution to achieve transparent interoperability between EGEE gLite and CNGRID GOS.

The activities to achieve higher level interoperability between gLite and GOS will be continued. We will complete the development and the tests of our solution. Upon completion of the testbed, we will start a full deployment of our solution on the production grid infrastructures.

From the experience gained in this work we can say that the major difficulty in middleware interoperability mainly comes from the data access issue. It is primarily caused by different data transfer protocols adopted by different middleware platforms, i.e. FTP in CNGrid GOS and GridFTP in EGEE. A special attention has been devoted and will be devoted in the next future to data management services in order to allow interoperable access to large data volumes across the two different infrastructures.

Acknowledgments

This work is partially funded by National Nature Science Foundation of China and EUChinaGrid project under EU FP6. We also thank Diego Scardaci, Giuseppe Andronico from Catania, INFN, Italy and other persons work for the EUChinaGrid project for their great help during our work.

References

[1] I. Foster and C. Kesselman. "The Grid: blueprint for a new Computing Infrastructure", Book, Ed. Morkan Kauffman, 1997.

[2] I. Foster, C. Kesselman and S. Tueckle, "The Anatomy of the Grid: Enabling Scalable Virtual Organizations", in *Lecture Notes in Computer* Science, Vol. 2150, 2001.

[3] I. Foster, "The Grid: A New Infrastructure for 21st Century Science", in *Physics Today*, Vol. 55, pp. 42-27, 2002.

[4] A. Shoshani, A. Sim, J. Gu, "Storage Resource Managers: Middleware Components for Grid Storage", in *Proceedings of the Nineteenth IEEE Symposium on Mass Storage Systems*, 2002.

[5] Storage Resource Management (SRM) Working Group: http://sdm.lbl.gov/srm-wg/

[6] Grid Security Infrastructure (GSI): http://www.globus.org/toolkit/docs/4.0/security/key-index.html

[7] EGEE project web site : http://public.eu-egee.org/

[8] EU e-Infrastructures web site: http://www.einfrastructures.org/

[9] gLite project web site: http://www.glite.org

[10] Grid INFN Laboratory for Dissemination Activities (GILDA) web site: https://gilda.ct.infn.it

[11] BDII (Berkeley Database Information Index):

[12] http://agrid.uibk.ac.at/wpa2/bdii.html

[13] Generic Information provider (GIP): http://vdt.cs.wisc.edu/components/gip.html

[14] JSDL (Job Submission Description Language): http://www.ogf.org/documents/GFD.56.pdf

[15] GridSAM-Grid Job Submission and Monitoring Web Service: http://gridsam.sourceforge.net/2.0.1/index.html

[16] CNGrid project web site: http://www.cngrid.org/ CNGrid GOS project web site: http://vega.ict.ac.cn/

[17] IoC (Inversion of Control): http://martinfowler.com/articles/injection.html

[18] Matt Welsh, David Culler and Eric Brewer, "SEDA:An Architecture for Well-Conditioned, Scalable Internet Services", in Proceedings of the Eighteenth Symposium on Operating Systems Principles(SOSP-18)

[19] OGSA-BES: https://forge.gridforum.org/sf/projects/ogsa-bes-wg

[20] JDL: http://edms.cern.ch/document/590869/1

[21] WS-Trust:http://schemas.xmlsoap.org/ws/2005/02/trust/

[22] EUChinaGrid project web site:www.euchinagrid.org

[23] K. Harrison , R. W. L. Jones , D. Liko and C. L. Tan "Distributed analysis in the ATLAS experiment," Proc. AHM Conf., 2006

[24] Grønager, M., et al.: LCG and ARC middleware interoperability. In: Proceedings of Computing in High Energy Physics (CHEP 2006), Mumbai, India (2006)

[25] Hidemoto Nakada, Hitoshi Sato, et al: Job invocation interoperability between NAREGI Middleware Beta and gLite. HPC Asia'07, SEOUL, Korea (2007)

[26] Bracco G., Migliori S., et al, "The gateway approach providing EGEE/gLite access to non-standard architectures", EGEE Technical Note EGEE-TR-2007-001

[27] Wang, Yongjian, Scardaci, Diego, et al: Interconnect EGEE and CNGRID e-Infrastructures through Interoperability between gLite and GOS Middlewares, Page

553-560, Proceedings of the Third IEEE International Conference on e-Science and Grid Computing

[28] Open Grid Forum Grid Interoperation Now Community Group. https://forge.gridforum.org/sf/projects/gin.

Realizing Interoperability among Grids: a Case Study with GARUDA Grid and the EGEE Grid

Asvija B, Shamjith K V, Sridharan R, Prahlada Rao BB, Mohanram N.

Centre for Development of Advanced Computing (C-DAC), India

Abstract

Recent endeavours from the global scientific and research community have resulted in realizing a massive number of customized, community oriented local and national grids. While each of these attempts has resulted in materialized frameworks that can successfully cater to a specific user community; this approach has daunted the vision of a single, unified, global, standards based Grid. Hence achieving Interoperability for the Co-existence of Grids with heterogeneous operating environments becomes the focus of today's research. This paper begins with a brief description on the need for inter-operability among world wide Grids, and further elaborates on identifying the exact requirements for achieving the same in Production environments with Functional and Operational perspectives. As a case study, specific challenges related to interoperation between the Indian GARUDA [1] Grid and the European EGEE [2] Grids, are discussed in detail. Possible approaches and solutions to address these specific issues at various levels are dealt at great length.

1   Introduction

Grid Interoperability can be defined as the "ability of components in a Grid to communicate and share, information and data to peer components in different Grids". Grids were evolved to support specific projects and applications in the field of particle analysis, disaster management & protein folding etc. These diversified project and application requirements led to the evolution of customized Grid Middlewares like, Globus Toolkit, Glite, Unicore, Gridbus, and Legion. So unifying all the grids to address challenging scientific problems and enabling application portability across the Grids became a necessity. Sensing this necessity OGF[3] made an initiative called GIN (Grid Interoperability Now)[4] to bring out certain area of work that needs to be addressed to solve interoperability issues in Grid.

S.C. Lin and E. Yen (eds.), *Production Grids in Asia: Applications, Developments and Global Ties*, DOI 10.1007/978-1-4419-0046-3_14,
© Springer Science + Business Media, LLC 2010

2   *Introduction to GARUDA*

GARUDA is a National Grid Computing initiative made by the Department of Information Technology, Government of India in November 2004. Currently GARUDA has aggregate resources of more than 400 CPUs and 13TB of storage with network connectivity between 45 organizations across 17 cities to provide seamless and high speed access to the compute, data & other resources in GARUDA. Figure 1 shows the architecture of grid GARUDA.

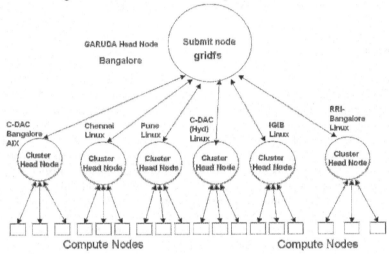

Figure 1 - Garuda Architecture

2.1   GARUDA Components

GARUDA components consists of its resources, resource schedulers, development tools & environments, data grid management solutions, grid access methods, applications, and grid management & monitoring solutions.

GARUDA grid resources constitutes of compute, storage and network resources along with scientific instruments, softwares and libraries. In the Proof of Concept phase of GARUDA, two applications of national importance, one belongs to Disaster Management and another one in Bio-informatics domain, have been deployed and executed to underscore the necessity and importance of a grid computing infrastructure.

3   Overview of EGEE

EGEE is the Project for Enabling Grids for E-SciencE Funded by European Commission to facilitate collaboration among research & engineering communities world wide, which aims to build on recent advances in grid technology and to develop a service grid infrastructure that is available to scientists 24 hours a day. Applications that are targeted in EGEE infrastructures falls in to different scientific disciplines, like High energy physics, life science, Geology, computational chemistry etc. The grid infrastructure in EGEE is primarily based a middleware called Glite [5], which is in fact build on top of the Globus Toolkit.

3.1   Glite Service components

Glite is born from the collaborative efforts from academic and industrial research centres as part of the EGEE Project. The Glite Grid services follow Service Oriented Architecture, so as to facilitate interoperability among Grid services and also to allow easier compliance with upcoming standards. The high level services in GLite middleware are Grid Access services, Security Services, Information and Monitoring services, Data services and Job management services.

4   GARUDA and EGEE Component Comparisons

To take a decision on the interoperability between GARUDA and EGEE, the middleware components that facilitate the grid computing infrastructure on both the grids need to be analyzed thoroughly. Main components that must be considered for comparisons are, Security, Grid Access Methods, Grid Meta-schedulers, Computing Elements, Storage Elements and Information services.

4.1   Comparison between Security Components

GARUDA and EGEE grids relies on the GSI[6] to enforce security. Users and resources in GARUDA and EGEE grids are identified by their certificates. In both grids the certificates comply with the X509 standard. GARUDA currently doesn't support VO based authorizations as in EGEE grid. The similarities and diversities in security components are given in the Table 1.

GARUDA	EGEE
GSI for authentication	GSI & VOMS[7] for authentication
Authorization based on Grid-map file	Authorization based on Grid-map file

DN is being mapped to local ac-counts	VOMS Attribute is mapped to Unix pool of accounts
Follows PKI based encryption	Follows PKI based encryption
Public Key length is 1024bits	Public Key length is 2048bits
Not recognized internationally	Recognized by IGTF

Table 1 - GARUDA & EGEE Security Comparison

4.2 Comparison between Grid Access Methods

In GARUDA, a grid user is allowed to access grid resources only through Grid Access portal. The Grid Access Portal takes care of submission and status monitoring of, sequential, homogeneous & heterogeneous parallel jobs. But, in EGEE the job submission is carried out using Glite UI commands. GARUDA Grid Portal provides interfaces to browse through the grid resources, where as in EGEE the same is accomplished using commands. Table 2 lists the different approaches followed in accessing GARUDA and EGEE grids.

GARUDA	EGEE
Through GARUDA Access portal	Command line UI
Job submission, monitoring and management interfaces available	Job submission, monitoring & management is done through commands
Facility to Browse GARUDA resources	Commands to list & search resources
Integrated with GARUDA Data Grid	Integrated with EGEE Data Grid
Provides GARUDA portal APIs	Exposes client APIs
Integrated with GARUDA Problem Solving Environment portals	Supports Grid Portals like, GENIUS, P-GRADE

Table 2 - GARUDA & EGEE Access Method Comparisons

4.3 Comparison between Grid Meta-schedulers

In GARUDA, MOAB[8] Workload Manager acts as the Meta-scheduler for the Grid. It accepts the job requirements in the form of MOAB script. MOAB is an extensive policy based scheduler, which has its components for both resources brokering and scheduling. Where as in EGEE the Work Load Management Service (WMS[9]) takes care of Meta-scheduling. Both meta-schedulers integrates well with PBS like LRMS. Table 3 matches the features and constraints of meta-schedulers in GARUDA & EGEE grids.

GARUDA	EGEE
MOAB is the Meta Scheduler deployed.	WMS acts as the Meta Scheduler
Moab handles both Resource Brokering & Scheduling	Does Resource Brokering & Matchmaking
Supports following LRMS • PBS • Torque • Loadleveler • LSF • SGE	Supported LRMS • PBS • Torque • LSF • SGE
Moab has its own logging & book keeping section.	LB [10] service responsible to store and manage logging and bookkeeping information generated by the various components of WMS

Table 3 - GARUDA & EGEE Meta-scheduler Comparisons

4.4 Comparison between computing elements

Computing elements are the components where the grid jobs will get executed and produces required output. Computing elements in GARUDA, runs RHEL and AIX operating systems. Where as in EGEE grid, computing elements runs only on Scientific Linux operating system, and there are some initiatives happening to support other Linux and non Linux operating systems. Table 4 shows the characteristics of computing elements in both GARUDA and EGEE grids.

GARUDA	EGEE
Operating Systems Linux (RHEL), AIX	Operating System supported is Scientific Linux, initiatives to support other Operating Systems are in progress
LRMS available are, PBS, Torque, Load Leveler, LSF, SGE	LRMS supported are PBS, Torque, SGE, LSF
Software installed are published into IS.	Software availability can be VO specific and advertised in IS
LB Host as part of Moab	LB Host is not hosted computing element.

Table 4 - GARUDA & EGEE Computing Elements Comparison

4.5   Comparison between storage elements

GARUDA extensively make use of the Storage Resource Broker (SRB [11]) from Nirvana, to accomplish the data management. Where as in EGEE data management is done using Storage Resource Manager (SRM [12]) and File Transfer Service (FTS). GARUDA data grid needs to have SRB credential for data management and transfer across the storage elements, but EGEE relies on GSI credentials for data management and transfers. Table 5 shows the comparison between storage elements in GARUDA and EGEE grids.

GARUDA	EGEE
Storage Resource Broker (SRB)	Storage Resource Manager (SRM) with File Transfer Service (FTS)
Provide a unified name space across the grid	Namespace Management catalogs LFC, AMGA
Supports only SRB Protocol.	Supports various data transfer protocols like Gsiftp, gsidcap, insecure, RFIO, secure RFIO
Require SRB credentials	Integrated with GSI
Provides command line, web and java clients	Command line interfaces are available
Exposes API's (C, JAVA)	Exposes API's (C,Perl)
GridFTP can be used to transfer files	GridFTP is used to transfer files
Supports file replication	Supports file replication

Table 5 - GARUDA & EGEE Storage Elements Comparison

4.6   Comparison between Information services

The Information System in GARUDA has been setup in a hierarchical manner to facilitate easy querying of information by different tools and users, and also to allow easy publishing of information from different information providers. Similarly, the EGEE grid information system also follows a hierarchical approach with Grid Resource Information Service (GRIS) at resource level and Grid Index Information Service (GIIS) at VO and grid level. The comparison between the GARUDA & EGEE Information Systems is shown in Table 6.

GARUDA	EGEE
Based on Globus MDS 2.0	Evolved version of Globus MDS
GIIS at Site level & GRIS at resource level	GRIS at resource level & GIIS at site and higher levels implemented through BDII [13]
Follows hierarchical approach for publishing information	Also follows a hierarchical approach

GLUE Schema[14] (v1.2) & GLOBUS Schema	Follows GLUE Schema (v1.3)
MDS 2.0 APIS	BDII APIs

Table 6 - GARUDA & EGEE Information Services Comparison

5 Interoperability Frameworks with GARUDA & EGEE: A Possible Advanced Scenario

A closer look at the existing EGEE and GARUDA Grid infrastructures reveal that interoperability between the two grids have to be achieved at various layers, in order to have a seamless access of resources between them. Each of the following layers listed below, need to be properly coordinated and modified to achieve seamless interoperability:

- Security
- Information Systems
- Job Management
- Data Management

5.1   Security Interoperability

It is evident that both Grids follow GSI for security, since GARUDA follows a private certifying authority which is not accredited by international certifying authorities, GARUDA resources and users need to get certificates from Internationally recognized CAs (Certifying Authority). Once the cross-certification has been done, EGEE resources will trust GARUDA resources and users and vice versa, so that they can be mutually authenticated. As the EGEE setup follows VO (Virtual Organization) based authorization rules, GARUDA users need to be part of a VO (euindia) that is recognized in EGEE. As GARUDA relies on grid-mapfile entry for authorization, EGEE users DN (Distinguished Name) will be mapped to local Unix pool of accounts in GARUDA resources. Through this approach Security Interoperability can be achieved.

5.2   Information Systems Interoperability

GARUDA tools have to validate & extract information from BDII of EGEE, where the information about EGEE resources are specified in Glue Schema. So, an adapter for fetching & processing information from BDII needs to be developed. Similarly EGEE needs to have an info fetch interface to access resource information from GARUDA Information System (GIS). As GIS is based on GIIS and in GIIS Information is specified in Glue Schema, an Info Fetch Interface needs to be developed for EGEE resources to understand the pieces of information in GARUDA. Differences in the versions of the GLUE schema being used in both the grids have to be addressed by the adapters to achieve the interoperability.

5.3   Job Submission Interoperability: EGEE to GARUDA

In EGEE grid, users submit their job requests using Glite UI commands. The requests are expressed using the Job Description Language (JDL) and will be submitted to the WMS. WMS components take the responsibility of matching the job request with that of suitable resources available in GARUDA. In order to accomplish this process, an Information Adapter for WMS + RB need to be developed to query GARUDA Information System. Once the suitable match has been found in GARUDA Grid, the adapter will be used to convert JDL to corresponding MOAB/RSL script with the data staging information. And the converted MOAB/RSL script will be used to submit the job to GARUDA. After submission, the job details will be updated in the Logging & Book keeping part of EGEE, and this info will be used to get the status and output of the submitted job. Figure 2 below shows the flow of job submission from EGEE to GARUDA.

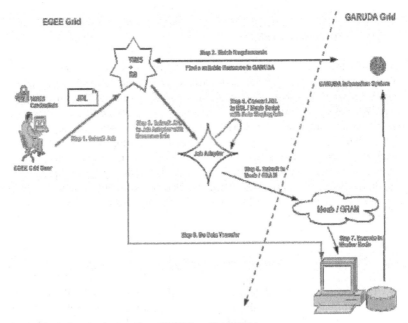

Figure 2 - Job submission from EGEE to GARUDA

5.4   Job Submission Interoperability: GARUDA to EGEE

Job submission from GARUDA to EGEE follows the same approach that of the job submission from EGEE to GARUDA. Garuda users submits Job Request through the Grid Access Portal, which in turn provides the user job request to Moab or Globus GRAM depending on the user requirements and type of the job. The job request will be matched with suitable resources in EGEE, in order to carryout this Information Adapter for Moab/ GRAM to query BDII need to be developed. Once the required match has been found, the job request need to be converted to corresponding job description language (JDL)[15] with data staging information, to carryout this functionality an adapter for converting Moab/ RSL [16] scripts to JDL need to be developed. After converting the job request to JDL, the adapter will take care of submitting jobs to the Workload Management Service (WMS) in EGEE and returns the job identifier. Using the job identifier GARUDA Grid Access Portal need to query the LB Service of EGEE to get the status and fetching the job output.

5.5   Data Management Interoperability: EGEE & GARUDA

Data Management in the EGEE is done using the Storage Resource Manager (SRM) and File Transfer Service (FTS). Where as Data Management in the GARUDA grid is accomplished using the Storage Resource Broker (SRB) from Nirvana Inc. As both the grids use fundamentally different components and technologies for accomplishing the data management, it is a harder task to achieve interoperability at the higher layer of Data Management tools. Academia Sinica (ASGC), Taiwan, is involved in developing an SRM (Storage Resource Manager) interface to SRB [17]. This integrated solution can be adopted to solve the data management interoperability in EGEE and GARUDA Grid. With this approach, the end users from both the grids can seamlessly access the data resources across the grids.

6   Conclusion

This paper described the methodologies need to be adapted to accomplish interoperability between GARUDA and EGEE grids with the existing setup. The Adapters and Converters required in information fetching, job request translation, job submission, staging job inputs and outputs need to be developed to realize the interoperability. Applications need to be tried for demonstrating interoperability between GARUDA and EGEE once the setup has been completed. In future GARUDA and EGEE need to adapt models based on OGF to realize the true interoperability.

References

[1]   The GARUDA Grid - http://www.garudaindia.in

[2]   The European Grid for E Science (EGEE) - http://public.eu-egee.org/

[3]   The Open Grid Forum (OGF)- http://ogf.org

[4]   The Grid Interoperability Now (GIN)
      http://forge.gridforum.org/sf/go/projects.gin/wiki

[5]   Glite - http://cern.ch/glite/

[6]   Overview of the Grid Security Infrastructure (GSI)
      http://www-unix.globus.org/security/overview.html

[7]   Virtual Organization Membership Service (VOMS)
      http://cern.ch/hep-project-grid-scg/voms.html

[8]   Moab Meta-scheduler – http://clusterresources.com

[9]   F. Pacini, EGEE User's Guide - WMS Service
      https://edms.cern.ch/document/572489/

[10] CESNET, EGEE User's Guide - Service Logging and Bookkeeping (L&B) -
      https://edms.cern.ch/document/571273/

[11] Storage Resource Broker - http://www.nirvanastorage.com/

[12] Storage Resource Manager (SRM) - http://sdm.lbl.gov/srm-wg/

[13] The BDII - http://twiki.cern.ch/twiki/bin/view/EGEE/BDII

[14] GLUE Schema - http://glueschema.forge.cnaf.infn.it/

[15] F. Pacini, JDL Attributes
      http://www.infn.it/workload-grid/docs/DataGrid-01-TEN-0142-0_2.pdf

[16] The Globus Resource Specification Language RSL v1.0 -
      http://www.globus.org/toolkit/docs/2.4/gram/rsl_spec1.html

[17] SRM interface to SRB Project -
      http://www.gridpp.ac.uk/wiki/SRM_SRB_interoperability

Uniform Access to Heterogeneous Grid Infrastructures with JSAGA

Sylvain Reynaud

CNRS/IN2P3 Computing Centre, France

Abstract

Grids have been developed to provide uniform access to computing and storage resources, but since existing grid infrastructures have been deployed within the context of distinct projects, technological choices have often differed. Many users need to use several grid infrastructures, and they are facing complexity because of these differences.

Several existing tools hide the middleware heterogeneity for this very purpose. However, the existing infrastructures do not differ only by their middleware; they also differ by their policies (e.g. network filtering rules), the supported security contexts (e.g. known certificate authorities) and the worker nodes configuration (e.g. available commands and services, environment variables).

This paper explains how JSAGA, an implementation of the OGF SAGA (Simple API for Grid Application) specification[8], addresses these issues to enable efficient and uniform usage of existing grid infrastructures, such as EGEE[12], OSG[13], DEISA[14], NAREGI[15]...

1. Introduction

1.1 Motivations

To increase the number of potentially available hardware resources is an obvious motivation for using several grid infrastructures, but it is not the only one.

Many users have potential access to several infrastructures of various scales, such as international, national or regional grids, as well as other distributed systems, such as local resource management systems, super-computers or standard computers. They may also be authorized to use infrastructures targeting different communities; academics or industrials, research or production.

All these infrastructures have different strengths and weaknesses. They have different overheads, performances, qualities of service, costs. They give access to hardware resources that have different characteristics and that are available in different quantities. For example, grids represent a significant source of computational power, but "this does not imply that traditional high-performance computers are obsolete. Many problems require tightly coupled computers, with low latencies and high communication bandwidths."[1].

The computational power provided by a single local computer dedicated to an application is negligible compared to the power of the grid. However, since it avoids wasting time in queues and other overheads, it can for example be used to run a job, which consolidates the results of other jobs submitted on the grid. It can also be useful for running interactive jobs or for debugging.

Some software resources may be bound to a given infrastructure because of their licensing restrictions. Hence, jobs requiring this software can not run on other infrastructures. When confidential data is used, user would select the resource, according to his trust in its owner, in the security policy and in the middleware.

Users accessing several types of infrastructures may select the most appropriate to perform a given task, according to criteria such as the task requirements, the deadline, the budget, the current load of each infrastructure, the usage restrictions stated in the licensing agreement of software used, the confidentiality of the data used or produced by this task, and sometimes the confidentiality of actions performed by the task.

No single existing infrastructure can match all these requirements at the same time, and users having different use-cases would take advantage of using several infrastructures. However, the complexity induced by the heterogeneity of existing infrastructures often discourages them to do so.

1.2   Overview

CNRS/IN2P3 Computing Centre (CC-IN2P3) is developing JSAGA[2] in the context of the project IGTMD (Grid Interoperability and Massive Data Transfer), funded by the ANR (French National Research Agency). The goal of JSAGA is to enable uniform access to existing infrastructures, and in particular to allow submitting jobs to several heterogeneous infrastructures with a single description of these jobs.

Its global architecture is composed of several layers (see figure 1), each layer being responsible for reducing the heterogeneity of the under-layer. The top and bottom layer, respectively "Grid applications" and "Legacy APIs", are not part of JSAGA and will not be covered in this paper. The "JSAGA plug-ins" layer provides access to existing infrastructure through a low-level but almost uniform set of interfaces. Within this layer, heterogeneity of interfaces is still present, but it is reduced to a limited number of interfaces per functionality. The "JSAGA core engine" layer provides a higher-level interface and completely hides the heterogeneity of middlewares. Finally, the "jobs collection management" layer deals with the heterogeneity of infrastructures.

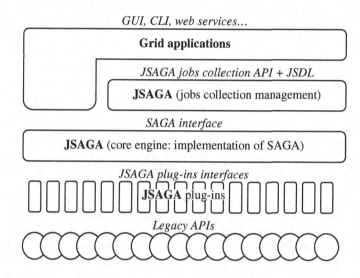

Fig. 1: Global architecture

In the next section, we present existing work related to grid interoperability. The organization of the rest of this paper is close to this architecture; Section 3 explains how we deal with heterogeneity of middlewares by describing the "JSAGA core engine" and its plug-ins. Section 4 explains how we deal with the heterogeneity of grid infrastructures by outlining the "jobs collection management" module. Finally, we present the conclusion and perspectives of this work.

2.1 *Related work*

Uniform access will be enabled between some of the national and international academic grids, thanks to interoperability projects such as GIN (Grid Interoperability Now)[3] and OMII-Europe[4]. In order to enable job submission to several grids in a uniform way, these projects are modifying some server components of the middleware. GIN enables modified server components in order to forward jobs to another grid, while OMII-Europe adds standard interfaces to these components.

Enabling grid interoperability by modifying server components has several benefits, but it is incompatible with our goal, which is to enable uniform access to existing infrastructures of various scales and communities. Indeed, we can not foresee neither modifying an international academic grid middleware to make it aware of a regional industrial grid (GIN approach), nor modifying every infrastructure we want to use to add them standard interfaces (OMII-Europe approach). Moreover, since these approaches are sensitive to deployment constraints, results are not expected in a short-term perspective, especially for large infrastructures such as international grids.

Nevertheless, these approaches are complementary to the one chosen for JSAGA. Indeed, JSAGA enables uniform access in a short time perspective, and it will benefit from the result of these grid interoperability projects to simplify its own code.

GAT[5] and CoG-Kit[6] hide middleware heterogeneity using the same approach as JSAGA; client-side encapsulation. However, the existing infrastructures do not differ only by their middleware; they also differ by their policies (e.g. network filtering rules), the supported security contexts (e.g. known certificate authorities) and the worker nodes configuration (e.g. available commands and services, environment variables). Hence, even if they are accessible through the same interface, separate infrastructures can generally not be used in the same way. These projects do not deal with this kind of heterogeneity; the infrastructure heterogeneity. Nevertheless, the SAGA specification benefits from the experience gained within these projects, as the research group in charge of its definition has worked closely with them[7].

The Simple API for Grid Applications (SAGA)[8] is an Application Programming Interface (API) specified by the Open Grid Forum (OGF) community. It addresses the gap between existing grid middleware and application-level needs by "providing a simple, stable, and uniform programming interface that integrates the most common grid programming abstractions"[7]. Simplicity is achieved by following the 80:20-Rule[3] in design, stability is achieved by standardization, and uniformity is achieved by providing a common interface, which is independent of any existing middleware. SAGA does not only hide heterogeneity of middlewares, it also shields the details of lower level middleware and system issues, and hides potential changes in their interfaces. Finally, SAGA provides similar semantics and style across commonly used functional requirements.
These are the reasons why we have chosen to implement this specification in JSAGA.

---

[3] "Design an API with 20% effort, and serve 80% of the application use cases"[7]

3.1 *Dealing with heterogeneity of grid middleware*

The first and most obvious difficulty users are facing when using several grid infrastructures is the heterogeneity of their middleware. To hide this heterogeneity, we need a common interface, which enables the user to express his requests in a middleware independent way. SAGA effectively fulfils this requirement.

JSAGA implements the functional packages defined by SAGA for security, data management and execution management. However, it currently does not implement its streaming and RPC packages because it would not serve our purpose. Indeed, our main purpose was to enable uniform access to the resources available through existing infrastructures, and only few of these infrastructures support these functionalities.

The purpose of this section is not to present the SAGA specification, but rather to explain the design choices we made when implementing the "JSAGA core engine" and its "plug-ins" (see figure 1).

3.1 Design approach

JSAGA is extensible; adding the support for a new technology is done by developing a new plug-in. SAGA is a language independent specification. Language bindings to this specification are provided separately for C++ and Java languages. JSAGA (Java Simple API for Grid Applications) implements the reference Java language binding of SAGA[9].

The SAGA specification is object-oriented, high-level and designed to match application developers' needs. It is easy to use, but it is not simple to implement, and the amount of code for the "JSAGA core engine" (see figure 1) is approximately twice the amount of code for all its plug-ins. Hence, re-implementing the SAGA interfaces for each supported technology would probably not be a good idea, and we had to define a lower-level set of interfaces for enabling integration of legacy middleware APIs to the core engine; the "JSAGA plug-ins interfaces" (see figure 1).

In JSAGA, these interfaces are service-oriented, low-level and designed to be close to the existing middleware APIs. High-level functionalities of the SAGA interface are implemented by combining the low-level methods of the plug-ins interfaces. For this purpose, middleware API exceptions, error codes, error messages and unexpected behaviours need to be converted to a set of well defined exceptions. Moreover, the approaches used by middlewares to solve a given problem often differ, and mapping them to the approach chosen for the common interface (i.e. SAGA in our case) may lead to an important loss of efficiency. The design of the plug-in interfaces does not only ease integration of new technologies, it also prevents this efficiency loss.

Some of the "JSAGA plug-in interfaces" propose several ways to implement each of the functionalities in order to ease integration of legacy APIs. For example, depending on the approach chosen by this API, job streams may be accessible before, during and/or after the job execution, though input or output stream objects. With JSAGA, each execution management plug-in implements the job stream interface, which is the closest to the legacy API. Then, the mapping of this interface to the common SAGA interface is done by the core engine. To make it accessible through the methods specified in SAGA (getInput, getOutput and getError), the core engine may have to redirect and/or to buffer the streamed data.

Some of the plug-in interfaces are optional. They allow implementing technology-specific optimizations and features. For example, while most of transfers are done using low-level read and write methods, an optional interface can be implemented to improve efficiency in some circumstances. This allows to use third-party transfer for protocols supporting it, or to move a file without copying it.
Some of the plug-in interfaces are redundant. A plug-in may implement several approaches for a single functionality in order to allow the core engine to select the one, which is the most efficient in the current context. For example, job monitoring plug-ins, which are distinct from job control plug-ins, may implements several job monitoring interfaces. While implementing only one interface is enough to monitor the job, implementing several, allows the core engine to select the most efficient one, depending on the user action and other on going monitoring activities. Job monitoring approaches include polling and listening for status changes, for individual jobs as well as for a set of enumerated or set of filtered jobs.

To improve performance, the core engine also allows reusing data management connections, and it keeps meta-data about files, as well as status of monitored jobs.

Unlike the SAGA interface, the "JSAGA plug-ins interfaces" do not completely hide middleware heterogeneity; they reduce it to an acceptable level of complexity, while providing appropriate control on the underlying middleware APIs for using them efficiently.

3.2   The plug-ins

JSAGA currently supports security, data management and execution management technologies provided by various grid middlewares, such as Globus Toolkit, Unicore, gLite, Naregi. It also supports more commonly used technologies, such as X509, HTTPS, SFTP, SSH.

JSAGA allows to uniformly use various grid (e.g. Globus proxy, VOMS, MyProxy) and non-grid (e.g. X509 certificates, Java keystore, SSH keys, login/password) security mechanisms. Each security context type can be initialized with several alternative sets of attributes. For example, a Globus proxy security context may be initialized by signing a certificate request with the user's certificate ("UserCert" and "UserKey" SAGA attributes) and its passphrase ("UserPass" attribute), or it may be created by simply loading the proxy file saved on disk ("UserProxy" attribute) if it is not expired. The plug-in set the default values from JSAGA configuration or by following the rules that usually apply for initialising this type of context. For example, for setting the default value of the "UserCert" attribute of a Globus proxy security context, the plug-in first checks the existence of the environment variable "X509_USER_CERT" else it uses a default path.

Supported data management protocols include both grid (e.g. GSIFTP, SRM, RByteIO) and non-grid (e.g. HTTP, HTTPS, SFTP, SRB, iRoDS) protocols. Most of them are either physical file or logical file management protocols, but some can be used as both, depending on which factory is used to instantiate the SAGA namespace entry object (e.g. SRB, iRoDS). The SRM plug-in[4] is implemented as a physical file management plug-in, and it uses the other plug-ins to perform the effective data management operations.

Plug-ins are provided to enable to submit jobs by using grid execution services (e.g. Globus gatekeeper, WS-GRAM, Unicore 6, gLite-WMS, NAREGI Super Scheduler) as well as by using commonly used solutions (e.g. SSH, fork). JSAGA internally uses the Job Submission Description Language (JSDL) specification[10] defined by the Open Grid Forum. JSAGA adds to it a few extensions, in particular for supporting data staging alternatives and pre/post-processing, and embeds it into a language designed to enable the description of jobs collection.
JSAGA provides two additional sets of plug-ins related to execution management. These plug-ins are not used for implementing the SAGA specification, and they are only available when using the JSAGA own jobs collection API. The first set of plug-ins translates job description from one language (e.g. SAGA attributes, JSDL, gLite-JDL) to the jobs collection description language internally used by JSAGA. The second set of plug-ins is for parametric jobs. It evaluates expressions included in the job description. Depending on the plug-in used, expressions can very basic (i.e. get the index of current job) or they can be more complex and contain arithmetic and string operations, date formatting, etc.

Of course, the main advantage of plug-ins is that you can develop your owns...

---

[4] At the time of writing this paper, this plug-in is still under development and not yet fully usable

4.1 *Dealing with heterogeneity of grid infrastructures*

This section explains the problem addressed by the "jobs collection management module" of JSAGA (see figure 1), and presents its implementation.

4.1 Problem statement

JSAGA overcomes the middleware heterogeneity problem by implementing the SAGA interface and mapping all the supported technologies to this interface. Figure 2 shows a use-case example; a job is submitted to both an international academic grid (EGEE) and a regional industrial grid (such as OpenPlast or RUGBI[16]). When submitting the job to the EGEE infrastructure, JSAGA forwards user requests to the gLite middleware and translates the job description into the Job Description Language (JDL). When submitting it to the industrial grid, JSAGA forwards user requests to the Globus middleware and translates the job description into the Resource Specification Language (RSL).

However, existing infrastructures do not differ only by their middleware; they also differ by their policies (e.g. network filtering rules), the supported security contexts (e.g. known certificate authorities) and the worker nodes configuration (e.g. available commands and services, environment variables). Hence, even if he or she accesses various grid infrastructures through the same interface, user will still not be able to use them in a uniform way.

Indeed, he or she will have to select the right security context to use for authenticating to the targeted grid. The security mechanisms enabling authentication could differ for each infrastructures, or it could be the same, but initialized with different parameters (see certificates on figure 2). The same is true for the technologies used for data management and execution management; both of them can be configured differently.

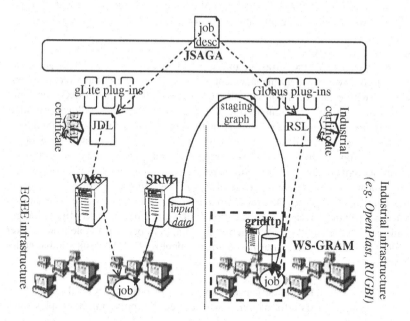

Fig. 2: Example of job submission on 2 grids

We also need to efficiently transport the job input and output data to, and from, the worker nodes. Transfer strategy depends on many parameters related to:

- the targeted grid or execution site; network filtering policy, availability of a close storage node, availability of a shared file system and access restrictions to it, data transfer commands, data files and applications deployed on the worker nodes.
- the protocols used; supported access modes, third-party transfer capability, security context delegation capability.
- the data itself; file size, possibility of sharing a the data file among several jobs, required data protection level.

The example of figure 2 shows input data that is directly accessed, using the SRM command line interface, by the job submitted on the EGEE infrastructure. This figure also shows that this input data has to be transferred to an intermediary storage node, which is accessible to the job running on a worker node from the industrial infrastructure, because this node has no outbound connectivity.

4.2 Describing grid infrastructures characteristics

A special feature of JSAGA is its capability to consider the aforementioned parameters when transferring job input and output data to/from the worker nodes.

For this purpose, we have defined a configuration language in order to describe the characteristics of the infrastructures available to the user. This language allows to configure security, data management and execution management technologies, and it structures this configuration into universes, grids and sites. JSAGA does not only have to support different security context types, it must also allow to simultaneously use several security contexts of the same type with different configurations. Hence, each grid is configured with its own security context. Universes, grids and sites can have a list of supported data management and execution management technologies, and they can be restricted to some domain and host names. For data management, the language allows to configure protocol-specific attributes, such as the number of parallel streams or the TCP window size. The same is true for execution management. Additional infrastructure-related configuration parameters include environment variables mapping, protocols available from worker nodes (depending on data transfer commands deployed) and default storage nodes to be used.

Moreover, some information can be provided at run-time, within the list of selected resources. This information is not required, but providing it, enables some optimizations.

Another information source is through the plug-ins. By implementing meta-data getter methods, plug-ins provide information related to the technologies; the base URL, default configuration attribute values and supported security context types. Thanks to introspection mechanisms, data management plug-ins also provide information about protocol type (i.e. logical or physical protocol), supported access modes and third-party transfer capability.

The knowledge base built from all these information sources is used for generating an optimal graph to efficiently transport the job input and output data to/from the worker nodes, while considering the constraints of each infrastructure.

5.1 *Conclusion and perspectives*

JSAGA implements two specifications defined by the Open Grid Forum: SAGA and JSDL. It has no prerequisite on existing infrastructure; it is able to use them as they are, thanks to the knowledge base described in the previous section. The design of its plug-in interfaces and implemented cache mechanisms, allow it to be efficient and scalable, even though it provides a high-level abstraction layer. Finally, the main asset of JSAGA is that it does not only deal with middleware heterogeneity, it also hides the heterogeneity of existing grid infrastructures. It enables submitting a collection of jobs to several heterogeneous infrastructures (e.g. EGEE, OSG, DEISA, NAREGI), with a single description of this collection.

JSAGA is currently used within different kind of tools; a web portal for industrial and academic grids (Elis@)[17] developed by the company CS-SI, a command line tool to submit efficiently collections of short life jobs on the EGEE grid infrastructure (JJS)[18], and a multi-protocol file explorer supporting both grid and non-grid protocols (JUX)[19]. The two latter tools are developed by CC-IN2P3.

Developers of these tools have also contributed to JSAGA by developing the plug-ins for the technologies they needed. In particular, British Telecom and CS-SI have provided an important contribution in the context of collaboration with CC-IN2P3 during the first semester 2008. All the contributed plug-ins have been integrated to the JSAGA distribution in order to be available to other projects.

Another collaboration has started with KEK computing centre in Japan, to enable the Japanese grid NAREGI usage through the standard SAGA interface.

Perspectives around JSAGA will be mainly to develop new plug-ins to support additional technologies. We also consider implementing the Service Discovery API SAGA extension[11].

References

[1]   Foster, C. Kesselman, S. Tuecke (2001) The Anatomy of the Grid: Enabling Scalable Virtual Organizations. Intl J. Supercomputer Applications.

[2]   JSAGA web site, http://grid.in2p3.fr/jsaga/
        Accessed 26 September 2008.

[3]   Grid Interoperability Now (GIN), http://forge.ggf.org/sf/go/projects.gin/wiki
        Accessed 26 September 2008.

[4]   OMII-Europe, http://omii-europe.org/
        Accessed 26 September 2008.

[5]   G. Allen, K. Davis, T. Goodale, A. Hutanu, H. Kaiser, T. Kielmann, A. Merzky, R. van Nieuwpoort, A. Reinefeld, F. Schintke, T. Schütt, E. Seidel, and B. Ullmer (2005) "The Grid Application Toolkit: Towards Generic and Easy Application Programming Interfaces for the Grid", Proceedings of the IEEE, 93(8):534-550.

[6]   G. von Laszewski, I. Foster, J. Gawor, and P. Lane (2001) A Java Commodity Grid Kit. Concurrency and Computation: Practice and Experience, 13(8-9):643-662.

[7]   T. Goodale, S. Jha, H. Kaiser, T. Kielmann, P. Kleijer, G. von Laszewskik, C. Lee, A. Merzky, H. Rajic, J. Shalf (2006) SAGA: A Simple API for Grid Applications – High-level application programming on the Grid, Computational Methods in Science and Technology, 12(1):7-20.

[8]   T. Goodale, S. Jha, H. Kaiser, T. Kielmann, P. Kleijer, A. Merzky, J. Shalf, C. Smith (2008) A Simple API for Grid Applications (SAGA) version 1.0.
        http://www.ogf.org/documents/GFD.90.pdf
        Accessed 26 September 2008.

[9]   C. Jacobs, T. Kielmann (2008) A Simple API for Grid Applications – Java Language Binding version 0.9. https://forge.gridforum.org/sf/go/doc15044
        Accessed 26 September 2008.

[10]   A. Anjomshoaa, F. Brisard, M. Drescher, D. Fellows, A. Ly, S. McGough, D. Pulsipher, A. Savva (2005) Job Submission Description Language (JSDL) Specification version 1.0. http://www.gridforum.org/documents/GFD.56.pdf
        Accessed 26 September 2008.

[11]   S. Fisher, A. Paventhan (2008) SAGA API Extension: Service Discovery API version 1.0 RC.1. http://www.ogf.org/Public_Comment_Docs/Documents/2008-05/saga_sd-v1.0rc1.pdf
        Accessed 26 September 2008.

[12]   EGEE, http://www.eu-egee.org/
        Accessed 7 October 2008.

[13]   OSG, http://www.opensciencegrid.org/
        Accessed 7 October 2008.

[14]   DEISA, http://www.deisa.eu/
        Accessed 7 October 2008.

[15]   NAREGI, http://www.naregi.org/index_e.html
        Accessed 7 October 2008.

[16]   RUGBI, http://rugbi.in2p3.fr/public/en/index.html
        Accessed 7 October 2008.

[17]   Elis@, http://elara.c-s.fr/elisaportal/servlet/Bienvenue
        Accessed 7 October 2008.

[18]   JJS, http://cc.in2p3.fr/docenligne/269
        Accessed 7 October 2008.

[19]   JUX, http://cc.in2p3.fr/docenligne/821
        Accessed 7 October 2008.

Part IV Operation & Management

Development and Operation of the D-Grid Infrastructure

Thomas Fieseler & Wolfgang Gürich

Jülich Supercomputing Centre, Germany

Abstract

D-Grid is the German national grid initiative, granted by the German Federal Ministry of Education and Research. In this paper we present the Core D-Grid which acts as a condensation nucleus to build a production grid and the latest developments of the infrastructure. The main difference compared to other international grid initiatives is the support of three middleware systems, namely LCG/gLite, Globus, and UNICORE for compute resources. Storage resources are connected via SRM/dCache and OGSA-DAI. In contrast to homogeneous communities, the partners in Core D-Grid have different missions and backgrounds (computing centres, universities, research centres), providing heterogeneous hardware from single processors to high performance supercomputing systems with different operating systems. We present methods to integrate these resources and services for the D-Grid infrastructure like a point of information, centralized user and virtual organization management, resource registration, software provision, and policies for the implementation (firewalls, certificates, user mapping).

1 Introduction to D-Grid

In September 2005, the German Federal Ministry of Education and Research started six community grid projects and an integration project to build up a sustainable grid infrastructure in Germany. More grid projects in the same context followed to join the common infrastructure. Currently there are about 20 projects [25] and additional associated projects.

The community projects are heterogeneous concerning the scientific field, the structure of the community, the structure and size of data being processed, the type of grid software in use, and the experience with grid computing. Despite all differences these communities are united by their common interest in grid methods for the solution of their scientific computation challenges. Some communities like high energy physics have wide experience with grid computing (HEPCG, AstroGrid-D), while others are just starting to apply the grid approach to their com-

S.C. Lin and E. Yen (eds.), *Production Grids in Asia: Applications, Developments and Global Ties*, DOI 10.1007/978-1-4419-0046-3_16,

putational tasks (TextGrid). Some of the communities which already applied grid computing intensively have a strong affinity to use a certain middleware (HEPCG – LCG/gLite, AstroGrid-D – Globus), while communities with less experience are still open in the choice of the middleware. The requirements of the communities in the grid middleware are highly variable, e.g. in applications of the HEPCG or AstroGrid-D comparatively few but very large data transfers are needed, while applications of TextGrid tend to have many transfers of small data sets.

In order to build up a common basic grid infrastructure for these heterogeneous grid communities the integration project has been started. The goal of the integration project is to build up a general, sustainable grid infrastructure, the Core D-Grid, first as a testbed and later as the productive environment for the grid communities.

In this paper, the structure of the integration project, its partners and resources, the supported middleware, and methods to integrate the resources into the Core D-Grid are presented. Services for the infrastructure like a point of information, a centralised user and VO management, a centralized resource management, software provision, and policies for the implementation (firewalls, certificates, user mapping) are described.

2 *D-Grid integration project*

2.1 Work packages

During the first phase, from September 2005 to the end of 2007, the D-Grid integration project (DGI) was divided into the following four work packages:

1. Basic grid software
2. Setup and operation of the D-Grid infrastructure
3. Network and security
4. Project management

These work packages have been introduced in detail in [13] and [14]. In the second phase, from 2008 to 2010, the work packages of the integration project DGI-2 are:

1. Support for grid users and resource providers
2. Operation of
3. Security

2.2 Support for grid users and resource providers

The work package support for users and providers comprises the point of information for grid users and resource providers, the trouble ticket system, and the provision of basic grid software.

2.2.1 Point of information

The point of information (POI) is divided into different sections, a section with general information about D-Grid and the community projects [6], a section with information about the integration project [7], a user portal [9], and a provider portal [10]. The user portal is intended as a first starting point for D-Grid users. Users can find information about middleware services, i.e. installation and usage of grid middleware clients of the middleware systems that are supported within D-Grid, about the resources which can be accessed within the Core D-Grid, information how the user can get access to the resources like grid user certificates, creation of a new virtual organization, membership in an existing virtual organization, the status of the resources, and a link to the trouble ticket system of the user support. In the provider portal, resource providers can find the information that is needed to integrate a new resource into the Core D-Grid, as information about grid server certificates, installation and configuration of the grid middleware server software according to the reference installation, information about ports to be opened in the firewalls, integration of the compute or storage resources into the grid resource registry service (GRRS), and the integration of the resources into the D-Grid monitoring system.

2.2.2 User support

A trouble ticket system similar as the system of the EGEE project has been installed to organize the user support [11]. In the user support centre, tickets are handled and forwarded to the next level of the user support, depending on the area of the user request. For community specific requests, each community must setup and operate an own consulting process. The partner sites (resource providers) must run a user support for requests concerning their site, and the integration project operates a user support for grid middleware specific and grid infrastructure specific requests.

2.2.3 Software provision

In the software section of the integration project, the basic grid middleware and further basic grid software are packaged and made available for the resource providers, grid developers, and grid users. Unlike other large grid projects as EGEE, which are mainly based on a single middleware, the requirements of the diverse D-Grid projects are too different to rely on a single grid middleware. Therefore, three middleware systems for compute resources are supported in the software stack of the integration project: LCG/gLite [22, 2], Globus (version 4) [15], and UNICORE (version 5) [28]. For storage resources, SRM/dCache [24], OGSADAI [21], iRODS [18], and JDBC [20] are supported by the integration project. Furthermore, GridSphere [23] is provided to implement portal solutions and the Grid Application Toolbox [1] is supported for application level programming.

2.3 Operation of the D-Grid infrastructure

The topics of second section of the integration project are the operation and the further development of the Core D-Grid infrastructure. Essential central components like the management of users and virtual organizations, the management of grid resources, and the user mapping process are described in detail in chapter 3.

2.4 Security

In the third part, security aspects of grid middleware and firewalls are considered and advice is given to the partners in the Core D-Grid and the D-Grid community projects. Furthermore, grid security topics like authentication and authorization are investigated in this part.

2.5 Data and information management

In this work package, grid methods for the management of data and information are provided and enhanced according to the requirements of the communities. This includes a further development of SRM/dCache, the provision of the Integrated Rule-Oriented Data System (iRODS) [18], and a standardized access to grid databases via OGSA-DAI and the Java Database Connectivity (JDBC) [20]. Furthermore, for the handling of metadata information a Resource Description Framework (RDF) [27] based metadata catalog system will be provided.

2.6 Development projects

In addition to the central services which are part of the infrastructure, this workpackage deals with the development and enhancement of further services that will supplement the central grid infrastructure. An accounting solution which is attached to the batch system and thus independent of the grid middleware system, support of customer relationship management (CRM), an enhanced support of the GridSphere portal framework, and an enhanced user and job centreed monitoring system for Globus 4 will be developed.

2.7 Project management and sustainability

The last section covers the project management, the coordination of the work packages of the infrastructure project, and the coordination of the collaboration between the integration project and the community projects. Furthermore, dissemination and legal and organizational questions are part of this package in order to create a sustainable infrastructure for e-science in Germany.

3   Core D-Grid infrastructure

For the operation of the Core D-Grid, different infrastructure components are required like a certificate infrastructure, a concept to install the three middlewares on one machine, a user and resource management system, resource monitoring, user support, and a point of information.

3.1 Certificates

The security of all three middleware systems is based on PKI and X.509 certificates. In Germany there are two certificate authorities for grid certificates, the Deutsche Forschungsnetz Public Key Infrastructure (DFN-PKI) [4] and the Grid Computing Centre Karlsruhe (GridKA) [16] which have been accredited by the EUGridPMA [12]. For both certificate authorities many registration authorities have been approved. All partners of the Core D-Grid and the community projects have setup registration authorities to enable an easy access of users and administrators to grid certificates. Since most of the D-Grid projects are parts of international communities, foreign grid user certificates issued by any certificate authority accredited by EUGridPMA [12] and IGTF [19] are accepted.

3.2 Resources

During the first phase of the project, grid resources have been provided by the partners of the DGI. This hardware was highly heterogeneous. The installation of grid middleware on less frequent platforms (e.g. Globus on AIX) and the integration of this hardware into the upcoming grid infrastructure was complicated but helpful to gain experience with different systems. At the end of 2006, the German Federal Ministry of Education and Research decided to invest additional funds for compute and storage resources located at partner sites of the Core D-Grid and the D-Grid community projects to serve as an additional incentive of the upcoming infrastructure. The additional funding was combined with the obligation to install all three middlewares for compute resources (LCG/gLite, Globus, UNICORE) in parallel on each of the new compute resources. All of the compute nodes of these clusters (about 20 clusters have been acquired) must be accessible via each of the three middlewares. Furthermore, at least one of the two middlewares for storage access (SRM/dCache, OGSA-DAI) must be installed on the storage resources.

Access to these additional resources must be granted to all virtual organizations (VOs) of D-Grid. Additional funds have been provided by the Ministry of Education and Research at the end of 2007 and 2008 for additional resources and a further enhancement of existing D-Grid compute and storage resources.

3.3 Reference installation

The request to install the complete middleware stack of the DGI on a single resource presently is a very demanding challenge, since the different middleware systems partially have very restrictive and mutually exclusive requirements (e.g. Scientific Linux for gLite worker nodes (WN) and even more restrictive Scientific Linux 3.0.x for the compute element (CE) on the one hand, the most up-to-date packages for Globus 4.0.x on the other hand). Since any solution to this problem is highly complicated, a reference installation, realizing the simultaneous installation of all supported middlewares systems has been set up [26]. This reference installation demonstrates how to run the different middleware systems on the same machine with access to all compute nodes by each of the three middlewares for compute resources (see figure 1).

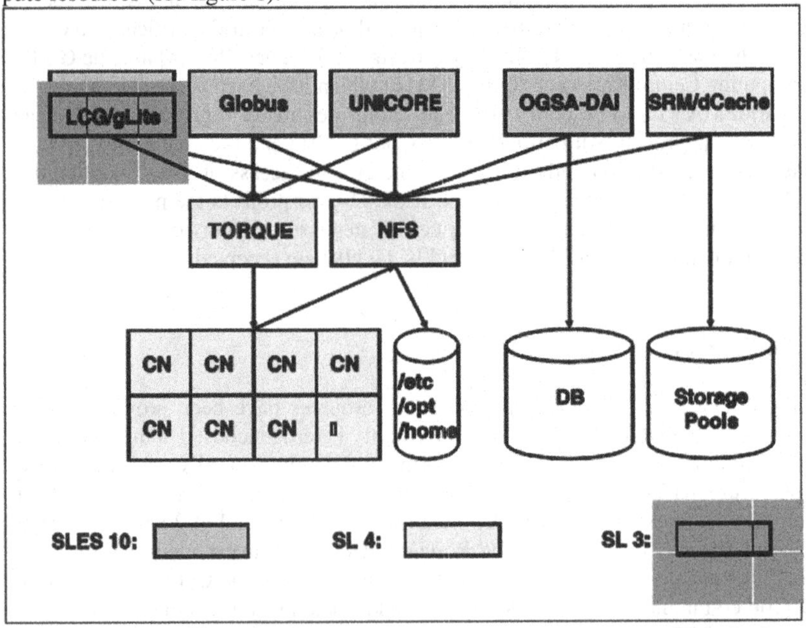

Fig. 1 Architecture of the reference installation. Jobs can be submitted via the frontend nodes for LCG/gLite, Globus, and UNICORE to the TORQUE batch system which can access all compute nodes (CN). Storage resources can be accessed by the frontend nodes for OGSA-DAI and SRM/dCache. The NFS node provides a common file system for configuration files (e.g. CA certificates), software, and home directories. The grey level of the nodes denotes the operating system.

For each of the grid middleware systems (LCG/gLite, Globus, UNICORE, OGSADAI, SRM/dCache) the reference installation provides a dedicated frontend node for the installation of the server side of the middleware. The operating system of the frontend nodes for Globus, UNICORE, and OGSA-DAI is SLES 10. The OS of the SRM/dCache frontend node is Scientific Linux 4, whereas the OS of the frontend node for the LCG/gLite compute element (CE) is Scientific Linux 3 (32bit) which is running on a Xen virtual machine under SLES 10. On the Globus frontend node, Globus Toolkit 4 is installed and the UNICORE frontend node runs TSI, NJS, and UUDB. On the LCG/gLite frontend node, the LCG-CE variant (production version) of the compute element is used. OGSA-DAI is I stalled together with Globus Toolkit 4 on the OGSA-DAI frontend node. The SRM/dCache frontend node runs dCache 1.0.7 of the LCG distribution. Two further dedicated nodes are used for NFS which exports common directories like the certificates of the certificate authorities, the gLite user interface (UI) software, and the home directories for grid users, another node is used for the server of the batch system TORQUE 2.1.6. The batch system server node is running Scientific Linux 4. All three middleware installations for compute resources (LCG/gLite, Globus, UNICORE) connect to the same batch system. Therefore, all compute nodes of the cluster can be accessed by all middleware systems. Another special node is dedicated for interactive use and can be accessed remotely by D-Grid developers and users via GSI-SSH or UNICORESSH. This node has the same environment (OS and configuration) as the compute nodes and can be used for software development and testing purposes. All other nodes are compute nodes running Scientific Linux 4. On the compute nodes, the client part of the batch system (TORQUE) and the gLite worker node (WN) software are installed. To submit further jobs within a running grid job, the gLite user interface (UI) can be accessed from the compute nodes via NFS.

Specially pre-configured packages of the middleware for the use within D-Grid are provided to ease the middleware installation and configuration for the partners.

The permanent development of the different components and grid middleware systems require corresponding updates of the reference installation, like the updates to Globus 4.2, gLite 3.1, and UNICORE 6 and upgrades of the operation system on worker nodes and frontend nodes. Therefore, a process for the ongoing development and update of the reference installation will be defined.

3.4 User and VO management

With an increasing number of communities, virtual organizations (VOs), and resources, an automated management of users and VOs on one side and of the resources on the other side are required to operate the grid infrastructure. The creation of a new VO is not an automated process in the present state of the integration project. Presently, this constraint is not a real problem, since the number of VOs is still manageable (currently 16 VOs for the community projects and additional VOs for testing and administration purposes). The creation of a new VO must be agreed between the managements of the community project to which the VO is related and of the integration project; one or more representatives of the new VO must be nominated. For each VO, an own instance of a virtual organization membership registration service (VOMRS) [29] is installed and configured on a central VO management server. A new D-Grid user must find a VO which is appropriate for his field of research. One of the representatives of the VO in question must agree upon the membership of the new member. If these requirements are fulfilled the new member can register to the VOMRS server of the VO (see figure 2, right side) and will obtain access to all resources of this VO. To meet the requirements of the LCG/gLite environment, the virtual organization membership service (VOMS) server is synchronized by the corresponding VOMRS server of each VO.

In some VOs information and programs should be shared within certain groups but must be hidden from other groups. To implement such a partition of a VO, groups within VOs are supported.

3.5 Resource management

In order to be integrated into the D-Grid infrastructure, each resource has to be registered at the grid resource registry service (GRRS), which has been developed within the D-Grid integration project (see figure 2, left side). During the registration process of a resource at the GRRS, all relevant information of the compute or storage resource and its administrators is collected and the grid server certificate of the resource is uploaded to the GRRS and stored in its database. Compute and storage resources which have to handle several middlewares (LCG/gLite, Globus, UNICORE, SRM/dCache, OGSA-DAI) simultaneously, have to be registered for each middleware with the grid server certificate of the frontend node of the respective middleware. For the administration of the resources, a client procedure (dgridmap [8]) is distributed to the resource providers and must be run regularly on the resource. The client contacts the GRRS server of the D-Grid resource management, authorizing itself with the grid server certificate for the respective resource (frontend node). On the server side, the VOs which are allowed to access the resource are determined as entries in the GRRS database. The corresponding VOMRS instances of these VOs are queried to provide the user information (DNs of the grid user certificates, ID of the user in this VO, etc.) of the members of the VOs. The result is the user mapping for the corresponding resource in the format which is appropriate for the middleware (e.g. grid-mapfile for Globus, input records for the UUDB administration tool for UNICORE). The naming convention of the unix accounts in the user mapping is $ppvvnnnn$, where pp is a prefix (default dg) which can be changed by the administrator according to the local requirements, vv is a short-cut for the VO of the user entry, and $nnnn$ is a number which is unique for this combination of user DN and VO. A member of a VO thus is mapped to accounts with name *ppvvnnnn* on all the resources of this VO, apart from the prefix *pp* which may vary between the sites. For resources with more than one middleware, the dgridmap client must be executed on the frontend nodes for each of the middleware systems.

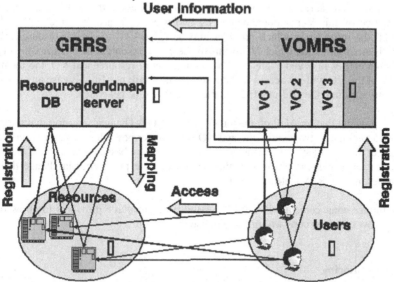

Fig. 2 Structure of the D-Grid user, VO, and resource management. In order to obtain access to the grid resources, users must register to a VO using the VOMRS instance for this VO. New resources must be registered at the GRRS to be integrated into the resource management. The user mapping for the resources is generated by the GRRS server which in turn obtains the information about users of the VOs from the VOMRS instances.

3.6 Extensions of User, VO, and resource management

In the implementation of the user and VO management as described in subsection 3.4 and the resource management as described in 3.5, the resource providers have to decide during the registration process which VOs are allowed to have access to the resource. This practice is adequate for the initial, more experimental phase of the D-Grid infrastructure, but will not be appropriate in the future when the tesbed advances into a production grid.With the steady development of D-Grid, more partners providing resources and more VOs using the resources will join the infrastructure. For such an evolving infrastructure a static assignment between resources and VOs is not sufficient, particularly since D-Grid operates a highly inhomogeneous infrastructure. Communities that collaborate with industrial partners are extremely cautious about the usage policies of the resources that they will use. Therefore, an enhanced user, VO, and resource management is under development (see figure 3).

In this new version, the users and VOs are still managed by VO specific instances of VOMRS servers. Each VO releases an acceptable use policy (AUP) for its members. On the other hand, each resource provider releases AUPs for each of his resources. The agreement between provider and VO about the usage of a special resource by this VO is implemented by two matrices P and V in the GRRS. P holds the information which provider allows which VOs to use his resources, V holds the information which VO wants to use which resources (see figure 3). Only if both entries in P and V are 1 for a combination of resource and VO, the members of the VO will get access to the resource, in detail: only in this case an appropriate entry into the grid-mapfile and the UUDB will be generated.

It is possible that an AUP of a resource or of a VO is changed, causing that a former agreement between provider and VO is no longer possible, or that vice versa a former disagreement can be changed into an agreement based on the new AUP. To permit such dynamic changes of the agreements, the providers can change their entries in the GRRS matrix at any time.

A further enhancement will be the possibility for resource providers to allow or disallow certain groups within a VO to use their resources.

3.7 Monitoring

Currently, monitoring is based on MDS and only available for Globus resources [3, 5]. On each Globus resource, the MDS4 software and a sensor transmitting additional information like the geographical coordinates of the site, the schedule of maintenance periods etc. have been installed. Each D-Grid resource provider is running a MDS index server for the site, collecting information of all resources of this site. The site index servers upload their information to a central D-Grid Web-MDS server, where D-Grid users can obtain the monitoring information in a hierarchical view, according to the organization levels of D-Grid. Furthermore, the resources can be displayed in a topological map.

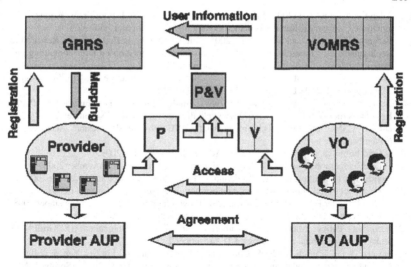

Fig. 3 Structure of the extended D-Grid user, VO, and resource management. GRRS, resource database, and dgridmap server are depicted as a single box (GRRS), the VOMRS instances for all VOs are depicted as a single box (VOMRS). The providers release AUPs for their resources, the VOs release AUPs for their members. Only if provider and VO agree on the use of a resource, both mapping matrices P and V have non-zero entries for a certain resource and a certain VO and the user mapping will be generated on the resource for the members of this VO. Even though P and V are drawn as separate boxes, they are parts of the GRRS.

The long-term goal is a D-Grid wide monitoring solution for all resources which is independent of the underlying grid middleware system. This monitoring system is developed in the D-Grid project D-MON [17] and will finally be integrated into the production grid infrastructure.

Acknowledgements

This work has been supported by the D-Grid Integration Project (DGI and DGI-2), a project funded by the Federal Ministry for Education and Research of Germany (BMBF) (grant numbers 01AK800F and 01IG070014B) as part of the D-Grid initiative. The integration project involves a large number of colleagues who all contribute to the project and the development of the D-Grid infrastructure.

References

[1] Allen G, Davis K et al (2003) Enabling Applications on the Grid: A GridLab Overview. International Journal of High Performance Computing Applications 17:449–466

[2] Berlich R, Kunze M, and Schwarz K (2005) Grid Computing in Europe: From Research to Deployment. In: Proceedings of the 2005 Australasian workshop on Grid computing and eresearch, Newcastle, New South Wales, Australia, 44:21–27

[3] Current status of the Core D-Grid Infrastructure. http://www.dgrid. de/index.php?id=209&L=1. Accessed 11 November 2008

[4] Deutsches Forschungsnetz (DFN). http://www.dfn.de/. Deutsches Forschungsnetz – Public Key Infrastructure (DFN-PKI). http://www.pki.dfn.de/. Accessed 11 November 2008

[5] D-Grid CSM. http://webmds.lrz-muenchen.de:8080/webmds/xslfiles/csm/. Accessed 11 November 2008

[6] D-Grid Initiative. http://www.d-grid.de/. Accessed 11 November 2008

[7] D-Grid Integration project (DGI). http://dgi.d-grid.de/. Accessed 11 November 2008

[8] Dgridmap Client. http://www.d-grid.de/index.php?id=335. Accessed 11 November 2008

[9] D-Grid User Portal. http://www.d-grid.de/userportal/. Accessed 11 November 2008

[10] D-Grid Provider Portal. http://www.d-grid.de/providerportal/. Accessed 11 November 2008

[11] D-Grid support D-GUS. http://dgus.d-grid.de/. Accessed 11 November 2008

[12] European Policy Management Authority for Grid Authentication (EUGridPMA). http://www.eugridpma.org/. Accessed 11 November 2008

[13] Fieseler T and G̈urich W (2008) Core D-Grid Infrastructure. In: Lin SC, Yen, E (ed) Grid Computing, International Symposium on Grid Computing (ISGC 2007), Springer, New York, 153–162

[14] Fieseler T and G̈urich W (2008) Operation of the Core D-Grid Infrastructure. In: 2008 Eighth IEEE International Symposium on Cluster Computing and the Grid (ccgrid), IEEE Computer Society Press, USA, 162–168

[15] Foster I (2006) Globus Toolkit Version 4: Software for Service-Oriented Systems. In: IFIP International Conference on Network and Parallel Computing, Springer-Verlag LNCS 3779, 2–13

[16] Grid Computing Centre Karlsruhe (GridKa). http://grid.fzk.de/. Accessed 11 November 2008

[17] Horizontal Integration of Resource- and Service Monitoring in D-Grid (D-MON). http://www.d-grid.de/index.php?id=401&L=1. Accessed 11 November 2008

[18] Integrated Rule-Oriented Data System (iRODS). http://www.irods.org/. Accessed 11 November 2008

[19] International Grid Trust Federation (IGTF), The Grid's Policy Management Authority, http://www.igtf.net/. Accessed 11 November 2008 20.

[20] Java Database Connectivity (JDBC). http://java.sun.com/products/jdbc/. Accessed 11 November 2008

[21] Karasavvas K, Antonioletti M et al (2005) Introduction to OGSA-DAI Services. In: Lecture Notes in Computer Science, Springer-Verlag LNCS 3458, 1–12

[22] Knobloch J and Robertson L (2006) LHC Computing Grid. The LCG TDR Editorial Board. http://lcg.web.cern.ch/LCG/tdr/LCG TDR v1 04.pdf. Accessed 11 November 2008

[23] Novotny J, Russell M and Wehrens O (2004) GridSphere: A Portal Framework for Building Collaborations. Concurrency & Computation-Practice & Experience 16:503–513

[24] Perelmutov T, Petravick D, Corso E (2006) The Storage Resource Manager Interface Specification. http://sdm.lbl.gov/srm-wg/. Accessed 11 November 2008

[25] Projects within the D-Grid Consortium, http://www.d-grid.de/index.php?id=41&L=1. Accessed 11 November 2008

[26] Reference installation of the D-Grid integration project, http://dgiref.d-grid.de/. Accessed 11 November 2008

[27] Resource Description Framework (RDF). http://www.w3.org/RDF/. Accessed 11 November 2008

[28] Streit A, Erwin D et al (2005) UNICORE - From Project Results to Production Grids. In: Grandinetti L (ed) Grid Computing: New Frontiers of High Performance Computing, Elsevier, 357–376

[29] Virtual Organization Membership Registration Service (VOMRS), http://www.uscms.org/SoftwareComputing/Grid/VO/. Accessed 11 November 2008

INDEX

A
Alice, 13, 49
Atlas,10, 43, 77, 158

B
Biomedical, 21, 102

C
CASTOR, 34, 71
CDF, 3, 49
CMS, 12, 59, 71, 79

D
deployment, 17, 30, 72, 117, 144, 171

E
EGEE, 4, 41, 61, 125, 155, 175

G
gLite, 10, 29, 41, 125, 155, 195

H
high energy physics, 6, 41, 49, 73, 125, 156, 177, 201

I
Interoperability, 9, 94, 155,175

L
LHC, 18, 29, 49, 59, 71,79
Life Science, 13, 107, 143,177

M
Monte Carlo simulation data, 37

N
network, 14, 29, 49, 73, 94, 118, 141, 157, 185, 200

O
OSG, 30, 54, 158,185

P
Parallel Computing, 16, 210

R
resource, 30, 41, 49, 72, 94, 129, 156, 176, 185, 199

S
Storage, 13, 29, 41, 60, 80, 113, 141, 164, 185, 199

U
UNICORE, 17, 158, 175, 199, 202
User Interface, 17, 53, 87, 102, 169, 205

V
VO, 10, 49, 60, 71, 109, 177, 200

W
WLCG, 59, 74